A SHOT IN THE DARK was first presented by Leland Hayward at the Booth Theatre, New York City, on October 18, 1961, with the following cast:

(In Order of Appearance)

PAUL SEVIGNE	*William Shatner*
MORESTAN	*Gene Saks*
LABLACHE	*Hugh Franklin*
ANTOINETTE SEVIGNE	*Diana van der Vlis*
JOSEFA LANTENAY	*Julie Harris*
DOMINIQUE BEAUREVERS	*Louise Troy*
BENJAMIN BEAUREVERS	*Walter Matthau*
GUARD	*Pierre Epstein*

SYNOPSIS OF SCENES

ACT I: The chamber of an examining magistrate. (Juge d' Instruction) in Paris. The present.

ACT II: The same. Two days later; morning.

ACT III: The same day, between five and six P. M.

A Shot in the Dark

A COMEDY IN THREE ACTS

Adapted by Harry Kurnitz

From the play "L'Idiote"
By Marcel Achard

No part of this book may be reproduced, stored in a retrieval system, or transmitted in any form, by any means, including mechanical, electronic, photocopying, recording, or otherwise, without the prior written permission of the publisher.

East Baton Rouge Parish Library
Baton Rouge, Louisiana

SAMUEL FRENCH, INC.
45 WEST 25TH STREET   NEW YORK 10010
7623 SUNSET BOULEVARD   HOLLYWOOD 90046
LONDON   *TORONTO*

Copyright ©, 1960, by Marcel Archard,
Under the Title "L'Idiote"
Copyright ©, 1962, by Harry Kurnitz

ALL RIGHTS RESERVED

CAUTION: Professionals and amateurs are hereby warned that A SHOT IN THE DARK is subject to a royalty. It is fully protected under the copyright laws of the United States of America, the British Commonwealth, including Canada, and all other countries of the Copyright Union. All rights, including professional, amateur, motion pictures, recitation, lecturing, public reading, radio broadcasting, television, and the rights of translation into foreign languages are strictly reserved. In its present form the play is dedicated to the reading public only.

A SHOT IN THE DARK may be given stage presentation by amateurs upon payment of a royalty of Fifty Dollars for the first performance, and Twenty-five Dollars for each additional performance, payable one week before the date when the play is given, to Samuel French, Inc., at 45 West 25th Street, New York, N.Y. 10010, or at 7623 Sunset Boulevard, Hollywood, Calif. 90046, or to Samuel French (Canada), Ltd., 80 Richmond Street East, Toronto, Ontario, Canada M5C 1P1.

Royalty of the required amount must be paid whether the play is presented for charity or gain and whether or not admission is charged.

Stock royalty quoted on application to Samuel French, Inc.

For all other rights than those stipulated above, apply to Irving Paul Lazar, 211 South Beverly Drive, Beverly Hills, California 90212.

Particular emphasis is laid on the question of amateur or professional readings, permission and terms for which must be secured in writing from Samuel French, Inc.

Copying from this book in whole or in part is strictly forbidden by law, and the right of performance is not transferable.

Whenever the play is produced the following notice must appear on all programs, printing and advertising for the play: "Produced by special arrangement with Samuel French, Inc."

Due authorship credit must be given on all programs, printing and advertising for the play.

Anyone presenting the play shall not commit or authorize any act or omission by which the copyright of the play or the right to copyright same may be impaired.

No changes shall be made in the play for the purpose of your production unless authorized in writing.

The publication of this play does not imply that it is necessarily available for performance by amateurs or professionals. Amateurs and professionals considering a production are strongly advised in their own interests to apply to Samuel French, Inc., for consent before starting rehearsals, advertising, or booking a theatre or hall.

Printed in U.S.A.

ISBN 0 573 61538 1

A Shot in the Dark

ACT ONE

SCENE: *Chamber of an Examining Magistrate (Juge d'Instruction) in Paris. It is a fairly large room, picturesque rather than squalid, but in no way judicially impressive except for the large double-doors at Back Center, which are leather-covered, brass-studded, as courtroom doors are everywhere. These doors open into a corridor, and the bench on which waiting witnesses and accused persons sit is visible to the audience. Two large desks, piled high with files and other papers, face each other Left and Right. The desk at Left is that of the Magistrate, the one at Right is the desk of the Clerk. A chair between the two desks, facing Left, is for the witness. There are files everywhere, dominating the room. On the walls there are some travel posters, one of which represents Holy Week in Spain, with penitents in black and red cloaks. A small bookcase behind the Magistrate's desk holds a small law library, works in various bindings and sizes readily accessible to him. This is topped by a large Empire clock with a figure representing Justice.*

AT RISE: *The Magistrate,* PAUL SEVIGNE, *is alone. He is about 35. Horn-rimmed glasses which he wears for reading make him look older and give him a scholarly air which tends to recede when he takes them off. He is attractive and well-dressed, though the effect which he strives for (and achieves) is sobriety rather than chic. He is standing, leaning against his own desk and studying an empty chair between him and his clerk's desk. The Clerk,* MORESTAN, *en-*

ters. He is young—about Sevigne's age, in fact—but already hardened and cynical by his years in the service.

MORESTAN. (*Crosses to* L. *desk.*) What a lunch! Believe me, you were wise to stay here and work. (*Hanging up his coat, etc.*) Restaurants in Paris these days! The odds are worse than in the National Lottery. (*As* SEVIGNE *immerses himself in the books again,* MORESTAN *shakes his head, pityingly.*) *Still* at the lawbooks?

SEVIGNE. (*Apologetically, defensively.*) It's my first case—a murder.

MORESTAN. Murder! *That's* not the point. A case is a case. The police have handed you a suspect, haven't they?

SEVIGNE. Yes—the maid.

MORESTAN. All right. Fire a few questions at her, get her to sign a statement, then you clap her into prison and get on to something else.

SEVIGNE. (*Drily.*) Is that how it's done?

MORESTAN. Sure! I've worked on dozens of these. Believe me, it's the best way.

SEVIGNE. What about this? (*Picks up one of the open lawbooks, reads.*) "An accused person must be protected from any infringement of his or her rights under the law . . . from the police or from the law itself . . . this is the first and the most sacred obligation of an examining magistrate." (*Glances up at* MORESTAN, *replacing the book.*)

MORESTAN. (*With a sigh.*) Well, if you believe everything you read— (*With a helpless gesture; crosses to* SEVIGNE.) Let's have a look at the summary of the evidence from the police.

SEVIGNE. Sure—right here— (*He fumbles in his file for the appropriate paper.*)

MORESTAN. (*Pained.*) In an interrogation, don't fumble for papers like that. The witness may get the idea that you're not sure of yourself. Here—let me show you. (SEVIGNE *surrenders the file,* MORESTAN *demonstrates.*)

ACT I   A SHOT IN THE DARK   7

Locate the document in advance, keep your finger on it, then *whip* it out! (*Which he does with a flourish.*)

SEVIGNE. (*Intrigued.*) That's not bad—let me try that— (*He takes the file from* MORESTAN.)

MORESTAN. I'm the witness— (*Seating himself in the chair.*) Go on—give me the works. Don't spare me! (SEVIGNE, *holding the file, is already circling the chair with a panther tread.* MORESTAN *nods approvingly.*) Very nice!

SEVIGNE. Did you know that a loaded revolver was kept in the Rolls-Royce?

MORESTAN. (*Cringing.*) No—I didn't know that.

SEVIGNE. Ah! I intend to refresh your memory. (*He has located the document, now whips it out with such a flourish that he spills a half-dozen papers on the floor.*) Oh, Hell!

MORESTAN. Don't worry; it takes a bit of practice, that's all. (*He stoops to pick up the papers, one at a time. He doesn't crawl.*)

SEVIGNE. I'd better stick to my books, and what I know.

MORESTAN. No, you'll be fine—say, the girl was found naked?

SEVIGNE. Yes—she fainted after the shooting, still holding the weapon. The chauffeur was her lover, they quarreled violently, she shot him. (*Thoughtfully.*) There seems to be quite a bit of that in Paris.

MORESTAN. Only in the winter—people are cooped up together. Ah, he beat her up now and then, eh?

SEVIGNE. Yes, once too often, apparently.

MORESTAN. Well, there you are—a snap—nothing to it—practically tied up in blue ribbons for you.

(LABLACHE *enters.* SEVIGNE *rises respectfully to greet him, as does* MORESTAN, *who crosses to his desk and sits.*)

LABLACHE. (*Cheerfully.*) Good afternoon, Morestan. . . . (*Crosses to* SEVIGNE, *shakes hands.*)

MORESTAN. Good afternoon, Monsieur Lablache.

LABLACHE. Sevigne—I thought I'd stop by to see how you were getting on. Your first interrogation today, isn't it?

SEVIGNE. Yes—in a few minutes, in fact.

LABLACHE. It's that shooting in the rue de la Faisanderie, isn't it? The maid and the chauffeur making love in her room—outbursts of jealousy, and—bang! (*Shrugs philosophically.*) Well, can't expect them to watch television forever. (*Reaches for the file.*) Is this it? (*As* SEVIGNE *nods.*) May I? (*Takes the file, seats himself, glancing though it.*) Ah! Splendid! (*He beams with obvious and great pleasure.*) The maid was found on the scene of the crime—the murder weapon in her hand—very nice! (*Drops the file casually on Sevigne's desk.*) Congratulations, Sevigne! It's an open-and-shut case!

SEVIGNE. (*Uncomfortably.*) Well, *her* story is that the door opened behind them, a shot was fired in the dark, and she promptly fainted.

LABLACHE. (*Pained.*) *That's* her story? Well, warn her that if she sticks to that, she'll be guilty of murder *and* contempt of court! Really! (*Rises; meaningfully.*) By the way, that's not just my opinion—that's how the Chief Prosecutor sees it, too.

SEVIGNE. (*Surprised.*) The Chief Prosecutor? (*Indicating the file.*) Has *he* followed the investigation?

LABLACHE. Are you mad? Certainly not! (*Then, patiently; crosses to* C.) Do you honestly expect the Chief Prosecutor to concern himself with the case of a parlormaid and a chauffeur bouncing from bed to bed until one of them died from it?

SEVIGNE. I just don't see how the Chief could form this opinion unless he——

LABLACHE. (*Slowly, pointedly.*) The girl and her victim both worked in the household of Benjamin Beaurevers.

SEVIGNE. That's bank, isn't it?

LABLACHE. Yes, a bank. Tell him, Morestan.

MORESTAN. In Paris, *the* bank. Beaurevers Freres! Billions!

LABLACHE. And a fine old family! (*Respectfully.*) Before her marriage, *she* was a St. Maur de Pignarolles!

MORESTAN. A member of the Beaurevers family rode beside the King in the First Crusade!

LABLACHE. (*Approvingly.*) Just so. He was, in fact, the treasurer.

SEVIGNE. (*Uncomfortably, fingering the file.*) I see what you mean—

LABLACHE. Of course you do! Get a confession from the girl—a short one, if possible, and you'll be home in time for an early dinner. Good luck, Sevigne. Call me the moment you've disposed of the case and I'll pass the good news along to the top. (*With a nod to* MORESTAN, *he goes.*)

SEVIGNE. (*Angrily.*) You know, Morestan, the Beaurevers family must be very nice, kind people. After all, they could have tried the girl themselves, found her guilty and guillotined her in the kitchen without consulting *anybody!*

MORESTAN. The rich like things done their way. Otherwise, what would be the point of having all that money?

SEVIGNE. (*Slamming a book.*) Damn!

MORESTAN. (*To appease him.*) I know how you feel. But what's the harm? The girl is guilty, isn't she?

SEVIGNE. What if she is? She should be tried by a judge and a jury; not by the social register and a bank!

MORESTAN. You're taking it too seriously. This is a business, and it's the Chief Prosecutor who runs it—now, just think along those lines— (*The door opens and* ANTOINETTE *enters.*) Oh, good afternoon, Madame Sevigne.

ANTOINETTE. Hello, Monsieur Morestan.

SEVIGNE. Hello, Antoinette—come on in. (*She looks at him anxiously. He is unsmiling, apparently pent-up.*)

ANTOINETTE. You don't mind? I'm not interrupting something important?

SEVIGNE. No—I've just been having a law lesson— from the Chief Prosecutor.

MORESTAN. Er—why don't I slip out and get a notebook for you. (*He exits.*)

ANTOINETTE. Darling, what's wrong?

SEVIGNE. Nothing—now. (*He gives her a big smile.*)

ANTOINETTE. You're not angry with me for coming here?

SEVIGNE. You arrived in the nick of time.

ANTOINETTE. Your first case—I wanted to wish you good luck. (*She embraces him—warmly.*)

SEVIGNE. Antoinette!

ANTOINETTE. (*Holding on.*) Well, I need *something* to take my mind off apartment-hunting.

SEVIGNE. Read a good book, or take a cold shower.

ANTOINETTE. If you knew the kind of places I've seen. Dark, dirty halls; dingy little rooms—and we can't even afford those.

SEVIGNE. Paris is for tourists. In Lyons we had a beautiful flat. Modern, sunny, all conveniences—

ANTOINETTE. *What* conveniences? It was three hundred miles from Christian Dior.

SEVIGNE. There was that drawback.

ANTOINETTE. Darling, the best possible incentive to success for any young magistrate is an extravagant young wife.

SEVIGNE. That's not a law—only a rumor.

ANTOINETTE. I've been right so far, haven't I? Didn't I tell you that within a year we would be out of Lyons, and in Paris?

SEVIGNE. Homeless, but closer to Christian Dior. (*And then.*) Antoinette, what if I were no good here—and they shipped me back to the law library and my old job?

ANTOINETTE. Oh, Paul—no!

SEVIGNE. They might.

ANTOINETTE. Paul, what's wrong? What's worrying you?

SEVIGNE. I don't know. I'm not sure that I fit in here. They seem to do things differently in Paris.

ANTOINETTE. Oh, darling! (*She embraces him.*)

SEVIGNE. Well, not *those* things.

ANTOINETTE. It's just that you're new here—but you won't be for long. And you're a brilliant lawyer.

SEVIGNE. I'm not sure that's enough—

ANTOINETTE. It is for me.

SEVIGNE. I'm glad you dropped in. I needed you. (*He kisses her. They are separated by a knock.*) Come in! (MORESTAN *enters, the file reassembled, puts it on Sevigne's desk.*) Morestan, this is your office just as much as it is mine. There is no need for you to knock before entering.

MORESTAN. Thank you. (*With a smile.*) You've cut yourself?

SEVIGNE. Eh?

ANTOINETTE. (*Sotto voce.*) Lipstick. (ANTOINETTE *smiles unconcernedly at* MORESTAN *as* SEVIGNE, *embarrassed, dabs at his mouth with a pocket handkerchief.*)

MORESTAN. It's just about time for our first witness—

SEVIGNE. (*Briskly.*) Yes. Now, out you go, Antoinette. Find us a nice apartment. Ten rooms, four baths, a terrace—and for very little money. That's an order.

ANTOINETTE. Yes, sir. Goodbye, Monsieur Morestan—goodbye, Paul— (*She blows him a kiss, exits.*)

MORESTAN. (*Shrewdly.*) Feeling better?

SEVIGNE. (*Smiling.*) Yes—quite a bit.

MORESTAN. (*With a shrug.*) *My* wife depresses me. (*Gets up.*) Shall I see if the girl is here?

SEVIGNE. Yes, let's have her in. (*As* MORESTAN *starts for the door. Rises.*) What do you think, Morestan—the friendly, fatherly approach for this one?

MORESTAN. The silent treatment. Let her sweat for a bit. Chances are she'll break down and confess before you ask the first question.

SEVIGNE. Then by all means the silent treatment.

(*He buries himself in writing at his desk, first donning his reading glasses.* MORESTAN *opens the door.* JOSEFA *is seen sitting on a bench.* MORESTAN *beckons, she rises and enters.* JOSEFA *is very pretty, delicate-looking as one would not expect in one who until recently was a farm-girl. Her manner and speech are candid, never common or vulgar, though her voice is not educated or affected.* MORESTAN *points to the chair, and she sits down. She tugs modestly at her skirt, but it is much too short. She glances at* SE-VIGNE, *who is bent over his work, utterly ignoring her, then to* MORESTAN, *who is similarly occupied. There is a long silence, while she looks around at the meagre adornments of the office. Whatever the silent treatment is supposed to effect,* JOSEFA *is apparently totally unimpressed. She takes a package of cigarettes from her purse, extracts one, then fumbles about for a packet of matches. She finds it, strikes one, is just about to touch it to her cigarette.*)

MORESTAN. (*A bark.*) No smoking!

(*Startled,* JOSEFA *waves out the match, then with a patient, good-humored shrug, she puts away the cigarette, still holding the burnt-out match. She looks around for some place to get rid of this, still utterly ignored by the* TWO MEN *who are apparently deeply absorbed in their work. Finally she puts the match in her purse too. The silence is heavy, prolonged.*)

JOSEFA. (*To* MORESTAN.) Was it for today? I can easily come back tomorrow— (MORESTAN *looks up at her, a long, pitying look, then goes back to his work. Again the silence. She looks from one to the other, getting no sign of recognition. Chuckling; to* SEVIGNE.) The guard out there told me a funny joke. Two old maids own a drugstore— (*She happens to be looking at* SE-VIGNE, *he raises his head and gives her such a long, bleak look that* JOSEFA *stops short.* SEVIGNE *puts his head down over his work again. The silence again. Then* JOSEFA *smiles, as if at last understanding something.*) Oh, we're waiting for the Magistrate, is that it?

(SEVIGNE *heaves a deep sigh. The silent treatment is ap-*

A SHOT IN THE DARK

parently having more effect on him than on its intended "victim" and he abandons the gambit.)

SEVIGNE. (*Rising.*) I am the Magistrate.

JOSEFA. (*Surprised.*) You? (*She looks at* SEVIGNE *carefully, then just as appraisingly at* MORESTAN, *then shrugs in casual agreement.*) All right. (*And as* SEVIGNE *is about to speak.*) You don't look it. He's more the type. (*Indicating* MORESTAN.)

SEVIGNE. (*Curtly.*) You'll have to take my word for it.

JOSEFA. I didn't say it to hurt your feelings. I only—

SEVIGNE. Be still! (JOSEFA *clams up. Behind her back* MORESTAN *makes a cautionary gesture.* SEVIGNE *gets a good grip on himself, proceeds quietly.*) Your name, please.

JOSEFA. Josefa Lantenay.

SEVIGNE. Where were you born?

JOSEFA. Espoletto—in the province of Drome.

SEVIGNE. Your age?

JOSEFA. Twenty-four. As a rule, I don't look it, but these last two days—

SEVIGNE. (*Abruptly, interrupting her.*) Your occupation?

JOSEFA. Parlormaid. (*Glancing around.*) Incidentally, your office is filthy. (*As* SEVIGNE *exhales sharply in exasperation.*) It is. You should speak to the charwoman. I'm a parlormaid myself, so I know how easy it is to sweep under the rug or—

SEVIGNE. (*Barking.*) Don't wander from the question!

JOSEFA. Oh—sorry! (*But she is irrepressible.*) It's not healthy to work where there's a lot of dust flying around— (SEVIGNE's *stare quiets her.*)

SEVIGNE. (*Rises.*) Josefa Lantenay, I am charged by law, as an Examining Magistrate, for the Higher Court, to conduct an inquiry into the death by shooting of one Miguel Ostos.

JOSEFA. (*Before he can breathe and continue. Sincerely.*) Poor Miguel! I can hardly believe it. He was so alive and—

SEVIGNE. (*Cutting her off.*) *Furthermore*— (*And as she subsides, crossing* U. *in front of desk.*) Furthermore, I am empowered to examine witnesses and accused persons in this affair, to interrogate them, and, if necessary to confront them with each other. My findings may be a basis for the arrest and imprisonment of any person or persons sufficiently implicated, and my recommendations will guide the presiding judge of any subsequent trial. Do you understand?

JOSEFA. (*Cheerfully.*) I am innocent.

SEVIGNE. (*Barking again.*) I didn't ask you that!

JOSEFA. I thought I'd tell you—to save you the trouble of questioning me.

SEVIGNE. It's no trouble, I assure you.

JOSEFA. All right. Shall I tell you what happened, in my own words?

SEVIGNE. Certainly not! (JOSEFA *shrugs as if it was all too much for her but she is willing to go along.* SEVIGNE *has a momentary struggle to maintain his judicial calm.*) Above all, Josefa Lantenay, be absolutely truthful in replying to my questions. If you tell even the slightest lie—

JOSEFA. Why should I lie? I have nothing to fear. (*Chattily, confidentially.*) As my father used to say, if you're poor, there are two worries you *don't* have—pickpockets, and lawyers. (MORESTAN *chokes back a laugh,* SEVIGNE *looks at him grimly, then at* JOSEFA. *Contrite, timidly.*) I'm sorry. You're a lawyer, aren't you?

SEVIGNE. (*Crosses behind desk.*) Don't you also want to know if I'm a pickpocket?

JOSEFA. I'm sorry. (SEVIGNE *circles back to the desk, sits, glancing at one of the law books open there, refreshing his grip on the technique, also giving himself an opportunity to get the questioning under control. Then he turns back to* JOSEFA, *more composed now. Before he can speak.*) I'm sorry about what I said—

SEVIGNE. All right!

JOSEFA. I didn't mean to be fresh, or—

SEVIGNE. All right! (*She quiets down. Then he faces*

JOSEFA *again. He hesitates, in case she is going to blurt out something, but she waits quietly, smiles at him. The coast is clear.*) Are your parents living?

JOSEFA. My father, yes. My mother—? (*She shrugs.*) I don't know. I never knew her, or anything about her. (*Wistfully.*) Strange, isn't it? Generally it is the father one can't identify. (*She is serenely unaware of* SEVIGNE'S *impatience.*) Four days after I was born, my mother ran away with a railroad conductor. (*Wistfully.*) I guess I didn't make a very good impression.

SEVIGNE. Your father is a farmer—correct?

JOSEFA. And a wine-grower. I worked for him until Madame Beaurevers hired me. My father's vineyard was only two kilometers from their chateau. I was their parlormaid for two summers before I came to Paris.

SEVIGNE. The deceased, Miguel Ostos, was already in their employ?

JOSEFA. Yes—chauffeur. (*Warmly, at the memory.*) In his uniform, *he* was something. (*Then adding, sincerely.*) Poor Miguel! (*In her confiding manner.*) You know something—at first he didn't appeal to me at all.

SEVIGNE. Judging from what you were wearing at the time of the shooting, I'd say that feeling wore off.

JOSEFA. (*She tugs modestly at her short skirt, an instinctive gesture, looks reproachfully at* SEVIGNE.) If you think I *liked* being found that way!

SEVIGNE. How long before you changed your mind about Ostos?

JOSEFA. Not long—I didn't even know it was happening, suddenly I was in love.

SEVIGNE. In love? With the man who raped you?
JOSEFA. (*Startled.*) Who—WHAT?

(SEVIGNE *has flicked a paper out of the file deftly.* MORESTAN *gives him an applauding look.*)

SEVIGNE. (*Reading, crisply.*) Testimony of Emile Bremontier, Janitor. Referring to Ostos, you described him as

—and I quote: "That crazy Spaniard who raped me in my father's fields."

JOSEFA. (*Thinking.*) Actually, it was on the way home from there— (*And then, plaintively.*) Say, what have you got in that book?

SEVIGNE. On the way home from there? Then he did rape you?

JOSEFA. Well—rape—I wouldn't want to make any trouble for Miguel *now*—

SEVIGNE. Is the witness lying? (*Rattling the paper.*) Did you say that?

JOSEFA. I might have been mad at Miguel that day.

SEVIGNE. Will you please answer—yes or no?

JOSEFA. (*Troubled, uncertain.*) Is it important?

SEVIGNE. Surely you're the best judge of that. But since it seems to confuse you, let it pass. This should be simpler: when you met Ostos, were you a virgin?

JOSEFA. (*Startled.*) What's being investigated here? (*Looks suspiciously at* SEVIGNE.) I mean, Justice is one thing, but—

SEVIGNE. Answer!

JOSEFA. My father never even asked me such a question!

SEVIGNE. A few days in jail will make you more cooperative. Morestan, get the guard—

JOSEFA. (*As* MORESTAN *is about to rise.*) No. Don't. (*Sulking, though.*) Some questions! (*Then plaintively.*) You're sure you're the judge? (*Turning to* MORESTAN.) Is he really—

SEVIGNE. Morestan—the guard—

JOSEFA. No, no—please—I'll tell you. (*She takes a breath.*) Well— (*And then.*) This is all confidential, isn't it? (*And at* SEVIGNE'S *mounting impatience.*) All right, all right. What was it again—did he rape me, or—?

SEVIGNE. Read the question, Morestan, please.

MORESTAN. (*Reading.*) When you met Ostos, were you a virgin?

JOSEFA. Ah, yes, of course.

SEVIGNE. You mean, you were?

ACT I   A SHOT IN THE DARK   17

JOSEFA. I mean, I remember the question.

SEVIGNE. Once and for all, will you answer it?

JOSEFA. All right. You're in such a hurry to know, you'd think we were engaged. (*And then.*) You know how it is in the provinces—boys and girls working side by side in the fields or the vineyards all summer—cooling off with a swim now and then—getting warm from the work—nobody wears very much— (*Her fear and antagonism forgotten, she gives* SEVIGNE *her warm, sunny smile.*) You'd like Espoletto!

SEVIGNE. (*Drily.*) I don't doubt it.

JOSEFA. (*Very friendly.*) Don't go in July—it rains quite a lot.

SEVIGNE. Now, then, you and the deceased, Ostos.

JOSEFA. (*Pained.*) You make him sound so very *dead!*

SEVIGNE. (*Elaborately.*) Correction. You and Miguel Ostos. When? Why? How?

JOSEFA. When? Why? How? (*Ruefully.*) I guess I'm lucky you don't want *pictures.* (*Then quickly, at his impatient look.*) All right, I'm telling. It was in August, the second or third Wednesday. I'm sure it was Wednesday, because we both had the day off. (*Reminiscently.*) The heat was awful that day but at sundown it was better. We walked to the vineyard to say hello to my father, then back along the river. The animals were being driven in from the fields—there was a sort of haze over everything along the riverbank—

SEVIGNE. Please! I see the scene very clearly.

JOSEFA. I want you to understand how it happened.

SEVIGNE. I'll understand. Just tell me what happened.

JOSEFA. I tripped over a root. I grabbed Miguel to keep from falling and somehow we *both* fell.

SEVIGNE. (*Waits for more, but there isn't any more.*) As simply as that?

JOSEFA. It was our day off. (*And then delicately.*) The heat, you know, and to tell you the truth, I wasn't wearing very much. I mean, underneath. (MORESTAN, *intrigued, has stopped writing altogether. A look from* SEVIGNE *sends him back to his notes.*) Anyway, there we were, Miguel and I— (*Plaintively, as* SEVIGNE *seems to be waiting.*) Doesn't that give you the general idea?

SEVIGNE. You didn't fight him off? You put up no resistance?

JOSEFA. In that heat? (*Then warmly, tenderly.*) I cried a little bit afterwards, but that wasn't because I was sorry it happened. It was something Miguel said that broke me up. He lit a cigarette, took a long puff, and then he said: "Long live the mother who made you!"

SEVIGNE. (*Formally.*) I should point out to you—if Miguel Ostos did overpower you and force his attentions on you, that might appear as an extenuating circumstance in your favor.

JOSEFA. Forced his attentions on me. I like that. (*Admiringly.*) That's a nice way to put it. I'll remember that. (*And then, suddenly, suspicious.*) Say, why do I need extenuating circumstances?

SEVIGNE. One never knows—they come in handy.

JOSEFA. You don't think I did it, do you?

SEVIGNE. I have not formed an opinion.

JOSEFA. (*Relieved.*) Oh.

SEVIGNE. However, if you're found with a gun in your hand, and there's a body on the floor— (*Shrugs, letting her form her own conclusions.*)

JOSEFA. (*Earnestly.*) But I *liked* Miguel. You believe that, don't you? *Please* believe that much.

SEVIGNE. All right.

JOSEFA. (*Earnestly.*) Thank you. (SEVIGNE *turns to his desk, darting a quick look at one of the lawbooks.* JOSEFA, *meanwhile, addresses* MORESTAN.) He's nice. (MORESTAN *gives her a stern look.* SEVIGNE *moves to front. She turns back to* SEVIGNE, *who is facing her, file in hand. She makes a face.*) Oh-oh! That book again!

SEVIGNE. Ostos talked of suicide, didn't he?

JOSEFA. (*Unimpressed.*) Spaniards. They talk.

SEVIGNE. You didn't think he meant it?

JOSEFA. Him—suicide? A man who used to cross himself before he made love? (*In her candid, confiding manner.*) Oh, I never mentioned it to him. I mean, who knows what people are really thinking at a time like that. Me for instance, I always pretend I'm on the deck of a big sailboat, with seagulls flapping all around. Or sometimes that I'm on top of a big mountain, above the clouds— (MORESTAN, *fascinated, has stopped writing, altogether.* JOSEFA, *rambling on contentedly, becomes aware of* SEVIGNE'S *grim look. She dries up.*) Oh—you're not interested?

SEVIGNE. If you go on like this, we'll be here all night.

JOSEFA. Just *us?*

SEVIGNE. Just *you.* Answer the questions. Don't keep wandering from the point.

JOSEFA. Yes, sir.

SEVIGNE. (*He has had a chance for a quick look at the books. Turns to* JOSEFA *again with the file, sits.*) He beat you, didn't he?

JOSEFA. Well—you know—we were in love.

SEVIGNE. That's why he beat you?

JOSEFA. (*Proudly.*) Never when he was drinking!

SEVIGNE. (*From the file.*) Witnesses have testified that in September and October you exhibited bruises on your face, arms and body—marks of beatings given you by Miguel Ostos.

JOSEFA. (*Comfortably.*) It was just in a conversation —one brags a little.

SEVIGNE. You quarreled bitterly. (*As she is about to speak.*) Don't deny it! (*Tapping the file.*) Here is the testimony of neighbors who swear that your fighting disturbed their sleep.

JOSEFA. Ha!

SEVIGNE. What sort of answer is that?

JOSEFA. Neighbors! Our fighting didn't bother them. (*Chuckling.*) What disturbed their sleep was when we made up. (*A tender memory.*) Ah, Miguel, Miguel!— he had a terrible temper but he certainly didn't hold a grudge.

SEVIGNE. (*Keeping after her.*) In any event, your relationship was continuously violent—do you deny that?

JOSEFA. What else could it be? He was a Spaniard.

He'd sit half the night at the window, sometimes, without speaking a single word, then throw himself on me, tearing at my clothes. It was a great nuisance, I promise you, because sometimes he'd just tear and rip every which way, and I hate sewing. (*Chattily, confidingly.*) Strange, isn't it?—housework, cooking, I love all that, but for some reason, I detest sewing. (*Sensing his impatience.*) Oh, I'm sorry. You're getting annoyed with me.

SEVIGNE. If you would just avoid wandering from the facts, please.

JOSEFA. I knew it. I could tell from the look on your face. How often I'd see that same expression on Miguel, and the next minute, he'd clout me one.

SEVIGNE. It's a temptation.

JOSEFA. (*After looking at him appraisingly.*) No—you're not the type.

SEVIGNE. You're very perceptive.

JOSEFA. (*Simply.*) One learns about men—from men. (*And then, with a deep sigh.*) Poor Miguel! He had only two passions in his life— (*After a pause.*) the other was bullfights.

SEVIGNE. From time to time he seems to have gotten the two confused.

JOSEFA. Poor Miguel! You should have seen his room—bullfight posters and souvenirs all over the place. He even took a Spanish paper, for the reviews. Poor Miguel! Just last week he was all worked up about a corrida in Mexico City. (*She leans forward excitedly, one* aficionado *to another.*) Luis Miguel Dominguin, with Rodrigo bulls—the most dangerous breed—horns like sabers! Dominguin made the first few passes kneeling in front of the barrera, and he himself planted the banderillas. Then a great *faena,* and what a kill! A single thrust of the sword—to the hilt. The crowd went mad and the judges gave him both ears, the tail, and one hoof. Even in Mexico, that's a lot. (*In a small voice, cheering.*) Ole! Dominguin! Ole!

(*Then to* SEVIGNE'S *amazement, she bursts into tears.*

MORESTAN *looks up from his writing, then the* TWO MEN *regard each other helplessly.*)

SEVIGNE. Oh, God! (*As* JOSEFA *sobs on,* SEVIGNE *rises.*) How did we get to *this?*
MORESTAN. The silent treatment!
SEVIGNE. (*Roughly.*) Blow your nose! (*He is touched though.*)
JOSEFA. (*Sniffling.*) I haven't got a handkerchief.
SEVIGNE. (*Crosses to her, giving her one.*) Here.
JOSEFA. Thank you. (*She blows her nose quite vigorously.*) I hate to cry. Excuse me.
SEVIGNE. Go right ahead. (*He uses the interlude to turn back to his desk for a refresher course in criminal law, shaking his head, apparently discouraged. Then he turns back.*) Better now?
JOSEFA. Yes. I'm sorry. It was just—thinking about Miguel— (*Wistfully.*) Do you think—wherever he is *now*—there are bullfights?
SEVIGNE. (*Startled, then kindly.*) Bullfights? I don't know—maybe.
JOSEFA. Well—maybe at least a Spanish paper, with reviews. (*Offering* SEVIGNE *the handkerchief.*) I'm fine now. I won't do it again.
SEVIGNE. Keep it—you never can tell.
JOSEFA. No. I'm fine now. I won't need the handkerchief— (*Extending it to him.*) I promise you.
SEVIGNE. (*Ignoring the handkerchief; crosses back behind desk, sits.*) You knew Ostos wanted to get married? (*As she nods.*) To someone else?
JOSEFA. He got ambitious suddenly. This girl, her parents are rich. They own a butcher shop.
SEVIGNE. You weren't jealous?
JOSEFA. Of her father's money? A butcher shop, in a good location, that's something. And *my* dowry— (*She laughs.*) My father didn't know about me and Miguel until I was in Paris. Then he sent me a wire: *"Don't come home and all is forgiven."* Funny old Pop—

SEVIGNE. (*Sharply.*) Love or money, you knew Ostos would leave you?

JOSEFA. What could I do about it? (*Then incredulously.*) You don't think that gave me a reason for killing Miguel?

SEVIGNE. (*Mildly.*) It happens, you know—a woman scorned—

JOSEFA. (*Earnestly.*) You've got it all wrong. I kept reminding him about the money and telling him she was beautiful— (*Confidentially.*) Beautiful: just between us, a real dog.

SEVIGNE. So you were reconciled to losing him? It didn't bother you?

JOSEFA. What lasts forever?

SEVIGNE. Yet he died in your room—you were nude.

JOSEFA. Please! (*Tugging at her skirt.*) I'll tell you about that—it was to be the last time. His idea, not mine, but I thought, well, so what?—why not part friends? I mean, after all, I *liked* him.

SEVIGNE. Apparently.

JOSEFA. Poor Miguel! He was really in one of his moods. First he babbled in Spanish, then he cried—really broke down and cried—and when I tried to console him, make him feel better—*novares et centavos, puta, puta, puta*—suddenly he was tearing off my clothes, throwing them all around the room and cursing like a madman. (*Confidentially.*) Believe me, it's a good thing I wanted to part friends, or I would have belted him with an ashtray. I hate that kind of hurly-burly. After all, it's not something you do for exercise, is it?

SEVIGNE. (*Rises.*) Strange, isn't it? Ostos was leaving *you*, and by your own account, *he* was behaving like a jealous madman?

JOSEFA. Oh? (*She is slightly apprehensive.*) Well—he was funny in a lot of ways— (*She is off-balance, though, if only momentarily.*)

SEVIGNE. (*Crosses U., around down to L. of her; pressing his advantage.*) *Why* was he jealous?

JOSEFA. I don't know.

ACT I   A SHOT IN THE DARK   23

SEVIGNE. Did he have reason to be?
JOSEFA. I don't know. A Spaniard, who knows why he was jealous?
SEVIGNE. (*Quickly.*) Then he was?
JOSEFA. (*Rattled.*) It was foolish—I shouldn't have told him—
SEVIGNE. (*Hammering at her.*) Told him *what?*
JOSEFA. Poor Miguel! (*She is thinking hard.*) I told you I liked him, didn't I?
SEVIGNE. Yes—repeatedly.
JOSEFA. Well—I thought if he was leaving me, he'd suffer—thinking I was alone—so, I told him there was someone else. It was a lie, I admit that—but, out of kindness.
SEVIGNE. (*Admiringly.*) Just to make him feel better. There was no other man?
JOSEFA. (*Dramatically.*) How could there be? When I give my heart— (*Strikes the palm of her hand with clenched fist.*) I give it all! To the hilt!
SEVIGNE. You were so considerate? Even though he was going to marry Solange Duval?
JOSEFA. Solange! Only a butcher would name his daughter Solange!
SEVIGNE. (*Categorically.*) Ostos and the Duval girl went out together—*once*. He took her to the movies and she was hopelessly bored because all through the film he talked about you. And of his insane jealousy.
JOSEFA. Liars—all of them—test the scales in their butcher shop and you'll see what I mean.
SEVIGNE. Why was Ostos raving about his jealousy— of *whom* was he jealous?
JOSEFA. I don't know— (*She is getting cornered, and looks it.*) A crazy Spaniard—he was jealous of shadows—

(SEVIGNE *is holding the file and she gives it a pained look. Having unobtrusively found his place, he now whips out the document.* MORESTAN *gives him an approving look.*)

SEVIGNE. (*Formally.*) I confront you now with the testimony of Madame Marthe Herbeux—

JOSEFA. (*Interrupting.*) Who?

SEVIGNE. The Beaurevers' cook.

JOSEFA. Oh—Camel-Face.

SEVIGNE. (*Irritated, proceeds.*) Madame Herbeux, interrogated by Inspector Colas, of the police. (*Clears his throat.*)

Question: "Was Miguel Ostos jealous of Josefa Lantenay?"

Answer: "He was foaming like a fire-extinguisher."

Question: "Why?"

Answer: "He knew Josefa was unfaithful to him, but he didn't know with who."

Question: "Did he suspect one man, or many?"

JOSEFA. (*Outraged.*) What?

SEVIGNE. Be still— (*From the file.*) Answer: "One man. Josefa isn't really a whore—just bedminded."

JOSEFA. Well, at last—a kind word.

SEVIGNE. (*Pointedly.*) And finally this, from Madame Herbeux: "Only two days before he died, Miguel came raging into my kitchen. He swore he would get the name of the man Josefa was sleeping with, and then—Boom! —Boom!—it would be over quickly." (*Snaps the file shut ominously.*) The fact is, Miguel Ostos never dreamed of leaving you. (*Then, severely.*) You urged the butcher's daughter on Miguel Ostos because *you* were leaving *him* —had actually left him.

JOSEFA. He died in my room. And you're forgetting how I was dressed.

SEVIGNE. I'll get to that. (*Calmly, reading.*) The cook testifies that Ostos complained for six weeks that your door was locked to him.

JOSEFA. Between the book and the cook you'll drive me out of my mind.

SEVIGNE. All right. (*Snaps the file shut, puts it behind him on the desk.* JOSEFA *is wary now.*) The fact is, you had no reason to invent a lover—he existed. You discarded Miguel Ostos for another man.

JOSEFA. (*A hint of scorn.*) So *that's* what you're investigating?

SEVIGNE. Is it true?

JOSEFA. (*Evasively.*) If I tell you it all goes in that damned book. (*Defensively.*) I didn't mind coming here—I thought you suspected me of killing Miguel—I mean, after all, that's at least a crime—but all you ask me is what I did where—how—when—with who?

SEVIGNE. (*Sharply.*) No more digressions! Is it true? Yes or no?

JOSEFA. (*Defiantly.*) All right—yes, it's true.

SEVIGNE. Thank you. (*He seems content, goes on in a kindly tone.*) You may smoke now, if you like.

JOSEFA. You're being nice to me suddenly.

SEVIGNE. We're nearly finished. We have the motive now.

JOSEFA. (*Startled.*) The—WHAT?

SEVIGNE. (*Gently.*) Your motive for the crime. (*Calmly, reasonably.*) Josefa Lantenay, I charge you with the murder of Miguel Ostos.

JOSEFA. Good for you! Say, is this a full-time job you have here?

SEVIGNE. You were found on the scene of the crime, with the murder weapon in your hand. Only the motive was missing.

JOSEFA. As long as it's my motive, is it all right to tell me what it was?

SEVIGNE. The lover who supplanted Ostos. That was your motive. To protect *him* from Ostos' jealous rage. (*To* MORESTAN.) Have you got that?

MORESTAN. (*Admiringly.*) Every word.

JOSEFA. (*Plaintively, to* MORESTAN.) *You* look like a sensible fellow—you tell him this is silly—

SEVIGNE. (*Crosses to her.*) Pay attention to me! Stand up.

JOSEFA. Now, don't you dare lay a finger on me—

SEVIGNE. *Stand up!* (*She stands, crosses to* C.) We are now going to reconstruct the crime exactly as it happened.

JOSEFA. But you know all about that. (*And then, resigned.*) I knew this was coming—men! (*She starts to tug down the zipper of her dress.*)

SEVIGNE. (*Outraged.*) Stop!

JOSEFA. (*Hand on zipper.*) Oh? You *don't* want it exactly as it happened? (*To* MORESTAN.) Didn't he say "exactly"?

MORESTAN. (*Intrigued.*) As a matter of fact, he did.

SEVIGNE. (*Controlled.*) Sit down! (*She shrugs, fixes her zipper, sits down.*) What are the dimensions of your room? (*Crosses* D. R.)

JOSEFA. (*Deprecatingly.*) It's a maid's room—don't you know what they are like? (*And then.*) No, chances are you wouldn't— (*At his impatience, exasperated.*) I never measured it. I suppose it's about twelve feet long, eight or ten feet wide.

SEVIGNE. How is it furnished?

JOSEFA. A chest of drawers, small table, an armchair, a straight chair by the window—oh, yes, and a bed.

SEVIGNE. How big a bed?

JOSEFA. (*Coolly.*) Big enough.

SEVIGNE. You told Ostos that it was all over—that you had a new lover.

JOSEFA. (*Reluctantly.*) Yes, I had to do it. It seemed the decent thing to do. (*Eagerly.*) But I told him it was nothing, a passing fancy, just a little bit of foolishness—

SEVIGNE. (*Sits at desk.*) He didn't believe you, did he?

JOSEFA. At first he did because I swore by the head of my papa— (*Adding wistfully.*) Poor Papa! But then he started raving again. He swore he would find the man and kill him. He rushed to get his coat, still cursing and raving.

SEVIGNE. What did you do?

JOSEFA. Well, I couldn't chase him—I was barefoot. I told him to stop acting like an idiot and come to bed. (*Ruefully.*) It was my own fault for trying to part friends.

SEVIGNE. You didn't struggle with him for the gun?

JOSEFA. What gun? We were in my bedroom, not a shooting gallery.

SEVIGNE. (*Leans in.*) Now, be sensible and listen to me. If you struggled with him, to get the gun away from him, it could have gone off by accident. An unpremeditated shooting. Under the circumstances, hardly a crime at all.

JOSEFA. (*Plaintive.*) You've got this thing about guns—

SEVIGNE. You said a moment ago that he was rushing out to find the man—and kill him.

JOSEFA. With a knife! (*Pityingly.*) Really, you know very little about Spaniards.

SEVIGNE. (*Crosses* L. *to her.*) Not all of us have had your opportunities for research. However, what about Ostos' speech to the cook: he swore he'd find the man, and then—Boom! Boom! it would be all over. Does that sound like a knife?

JOSEFA. (*Trying it.*) Boom! Boom! (*Shrugs, candidly.*) No, it doesn't. (*And again.*) Boom! Boom! (*Gives up.*) You've got me there.

(SEVIGNE *is circling the chair, stalking her as he did the empty chair at the opening.* JOSEFA'S *head turns with him, watching him warily.*)

SEVIGNE. (*Crosses* C., *circles. Suddenly.*) Did you know that a gun was kept in the glove-compartment of the Rolls-Royce?

JOSEFA. (*Calmly.*) Which Rolls-Royce?

SEVIGNE. What?

JOSEFA. (*Patiently.*) We have three.

SEVIGNE. (*Startled, involuntarily.*) You have? (*Blinks, fumbles in the file.*) Let me see—ah, the limousine. (*Confronting her again.*) Do you deny it?

JOSEFA. How should I know what goes on in the limousine, or in the glove compartment? But in my bedroom, no guns.

SEVIGNE. Very nice. What about the gun that was found in your hand?

JOSEFA. *I* was unconscious.

SEVIGNE. Conveniently. (*Takes a photo enlargement from the file.*) Do you know what this is? It was made by experts in the police department. This—on the left—is a microscopic enlargement of a bullet fired from the pistol you had in your hand—this on the right is a similar study of the bullet taken from the body of Miguel Ostos—

JOSEFA. (*Involuntarily.*) Oh! How awful!

SEVIGNE. They are identical!

JOSEFA. What a disgusting thing to carry about with you! (*She covers her face with her hands.* SEVIGNE *pulls them down roughly.*)

SEVIGNE. Furthermore, you had in your hand a .38 calibre Biretta automatic pistol which has been identified as the gun kept in the Rolls-Royce— (*Adding quickly.*) And don't say *which* Rolls-Royce! Ostos took it from the car, brought it to your room, and when he threatened—as you yourself have testified—that he would kill your lover, *you shot him!*

JOSEFA. No! That's not true! I swear it!

SEVIGNE. (*Turns away* L., *puts dossier on Morestan's desk.*) By the head of your papa? (*Adding ironically.*) Poor Papa!

JOSEFA. (*Wounded.*) Oh! (*And then.*) How can you hurt me so?

SEVIGNE. You're lying and concealing information. That means I have to dig deeper. Don't blame me if I strike a nerve. Morestan—chalk! (MORESTAN *brings his chalk from the desk drawer. Meanwhile* SEVIGNE *turns to his books on the desk, nods approvingly at what he reads. To* JOSEFA.) Get up! (*She rises. He moves her chair* U. R., *leaving the space between the two desks free.*) Over there— (*Pointing to Morestan's desk. She moves obediently. Kneeling.*) Now, then— (*He draws a rough rectangle on the floor. He crosses* R., *then Down.*) this is the shape of your room—

JOSEFA. (*Crosses* L.; *to* MORESTAN.) Is he *always* like this?

SEVIGNE. (*Roughly.*) Pay attention. (*Crosses, then Up, completes room. Indicating the chalk outline.*) Show me the location of your bed. (*And as she hesitates.*) Now, don't be coy. It seems to have been a landmark as well-known as the Eiffel Tower.

JOSEFA. (*Outraged.*) Oh! (*Stamps her foot on* R. *side of the outline.*) There!

SEVIGNE. (*Makes an* X *on the spot.*) The chest of drawers? (*Sullenly* JOSEFA *indicates* U. L. *of the outline and* SEVIGNE *marks it with a small square. As he works:*) The window—here, on the street side—right? (*At* D. L.; *he marks it.*) The armchair, here, by the window—right? Now—the door? (JOSEFA *sullenly indicates it, at* U. L. *of the rectangle, and* SEVINGE *marks it. He straightens up, tossing the chalk back to* MORESTAN.) The pure science of criminology will bring us to the truth in this matter. (*Confidently.*) Now, then— (*Peers at his drawing but having made it he isn't quite certain what to do with it.*) Er—just study that. Fix it in your memory. (*Crosses* D. R. *While he turns to the desk for a quick flash at the books.*)

JOSEFA. (*At* U. C.; *critically.*) I like it. In the house they have funny pictures like that—*millions* some of them cost—and not a bit better than yours. (*At his cold, penetrating look—defensively.*) You told me to study it!

SEVIGNE. Now—think—were the lights in your room on, or off?

JOSEFA. (*Flatly.*) Off.

SEVIGNE. You're positive?

JOSEFA. Positive. With Miguel, it was always in the dark. (*Confidingly.*) Poor Miguel! You see, he couldn't get over thinking it was a sin. Maybe it is, but turning out the lights doesn't change *that* and the times I've stubbed my toe in the dark—

SEVIGNE. You're wandering again. No reminiscing, *please!*

JOSEFA. (*Wounded, but sweetly.*) But these are memories of love! They're important!

SEVIGNE. Another time. Now, just stick to the facts.

JOSEFA. Why don't you listen? It might take your mind off guns and those dirty pictures of bullets— (SEVIGNE *crosses* R. *a step. At his mounting impatience.*) All right, the facts. There we were. The door opened, a shot was fired. He fell, and I fainted. (*At* SEVIGNE'S *steady stare.*) Well, you asked me. (*At his pitying stare.*) That's what you wanted—facts.

SEVIGNE. Sit down! Who else had a key to your room?

JOSEFA. (*Sits.*) Nobody.

SEVIGNE. Then how did the door open behind Ostos just before he was killed?

JOSEFA. I don't know.

SEVIGNE. This happened in the home of the banker Benjamin Beaurevers. (*Crosses behind* C. *desk, sits.*) Now, honestly, can you picture unknown intruders prowling in the halls, opening locked doors, firing shots, vanishing like ghosts? That's a ridiculous story.

JOSEFA. (*Angrily.*) Sure, it's ridiculous. (*Rises.*) It's the truth, that's why. Do you think *I* like it? When I told it to Inspector Colas he took my temperature, he thought I had fever. I wish I could tell you a smooth, elegant story, but I'm telling you what really happened. I know it's terrible and clumsy, but it's the truth, and it's all I have.

SEVIGNE. Morestan, note that I am unimpressed by this outburst. Sit down! (JOSEFA *sits.*) What other visitors did you have?

JOSEFA. (*Still sulking.*) When?

SEVIGNE. (*Patiently.*) The night Ostos was killed.

JOSEFA. I'm not allowed to have visitors in my room— (*Then sheepishly.*) That *does* sound funny, I admit. But poor Miguel, I mean, he wasn't really a visitor.

SEVIGNE. Please answer the question.

JOSEFA. Oh—I thought I did. (*Her response is nervous.*)

SEVIGNE. Just a simple "yes" or "no" will do it.

ACT I   **A SHOT IN THE DARK**   31

JOSEFA. It's simple for you, but my head is spinning with questions—and answers—I don't even know which is which.

SEVIGNE. Is this really so difficult? (*She looks at him uncertainly.*) On the night of the crime, other than Miguel Ostos, did you have any visitors in your room?

JOSEFA. (*Cornered.*) No!

SEVIGNE. Thank you. So it narrows down to just you and the victim in your bedroom, doesn't it?

JOSEFA. It's a small room.

SEVIGNE. (*From the file.*) After the shot, you immediately fainted?

JOSEFA. Right away. (*With a snap.*) Like that!

SEVIGNE. You fell beside the bed?

JOSEFA. Yes. I can prove it because I've still got the bump from when I hit the bedpost on the way down.

SEVIGNE. Indicate the exact spot, please—on the diagram. (JOSEFA *rises, crosses* U. L.; *points to it. He marks the spot.*) Now, where was Ostos when the shot was fired?

JOSEFA. There. (*She indicates the place* D. R. *and he marks it. The diagram is quite cluttered now.*)

SEVIGNE. (*Annoyed.*) Very well. You and Ostos were about ten feet apart—is that right?

JOSEFA. Yes—I suppose so.

SEVIGNE. According to the police laboratory, the shot was fired from a distance of just about ten feet.

JOSEFA. Of course. I told you all along: the shot was fired from the hall, when the door opened.

SEVIGNE. Or from here— (*Indicating Josefa's place in the diagram.*) from the bed—exactly ten feet away—*by you.*

JOSEFA. Please! (*Then reasonably, pleading with him.*) I am in my bedroom. What would I be doing with a gun? *Where* would it be?

SEVIGNE. Anywhere. Under the pillows—in the bedclothes—

JOSEFA. You have a funny idea of what goes on in a girl's bedroom.

SEVIGNE. (*Drily.*) Perhaps. I daresay it came as a surprise to Ostos, too. (*Then, with a touch of formality.*) Are you acquainted with a lawyer who might represent you? (*Crosses U. R. behind desk.*)

JOSEFA. No.

SEVIGNE. You'll need one.

JOSEFA. No. I don't want a lawyer. (*Miserably, glaring at him.*) I know enough lawyers.

SEVIGNE. Knowing one more won't corrupt you. I'll see that counsel is assigned to your case.

JOSEFA. I tell you, I don't want a lawyer.

SEVIGNE. Don't be stubborn about this. Do you realize the trouble you're in?

JOSEFA. (*Sits.*) I'm choking on it.

SEVIGNE. There's more. (*His tone is reasonable, mild.*) Now, listen carefully— (*She is impressed, troubled.*) Ostos didn't die at once. He lived for a few minutes, and he talked.

JOSEFA. What? (*The cry is not for her own peril.*) Oh, no! My poor Miguel! He saw himself dying? (*She covers her face with her hands.*) Oh, why did you tell me?

SEVIGNE. Because he *talked*. (*Sits.*) Do you realize what that means? (*She looks at him timidly.*) In the presence of witnesses, he said: "Josefa, why did you do it?"

JOSEFA. (*In a shocked whisper.*) He died that way— thinking I had killed him? Oh, Miguel, wherever you are now, you know I didn't do it.

SEVIGNE. It is a powerful accusation against you.

JOSEFA. (*Shivering.*) I know. Poor Miguel—

SEVIGNE. Stop saying: "Poor Miguel"! His worries are over. Yours are just starting. (*Taking a paper from his desk.*) Do you know what this is? (*Rises.*) A warrant for your arrest. The guard is waiting outside there to take you to prison. The next step is trial, then prison again— *or worse.*

JOSEFA. (*An outburst.*) Why? Do I look like a killer, or sound like one? Miguel and I were lovers once, and he was still dear to me. *Why* would I kill him?

SEVIGNE. (*Crosses Down to her.*) I told you why. To protect someone. The man you love now.

JOSEFA. I swear that's not true!

SEVIGNE. (*Attacking.*) Then give me his name! (*She stiffens at once.*) Come on—out with it—quickly—the name of the man!

(*A tense moment of silence.*)

JOSEFA. (*Quietly.*) If the warrant is ready, I'm ready.

(SEVIGNE *studies her, she drops her eyes.*)

SEVIGNE. (*Speculating.*) Suddenly, you're hard, and determined.

JOSEFA. Can't I just go to prison,—without speeches?

SEVIGNE. You won't give me the name of the man?

JOSEFA. No!

SEVIGNE. And you say you couldn't have killed Ostos to protect this man? When right here and now you're risking everything for him?

JOSEFA. That's my affair.

SEVIGNE. Mine, too. Because it proves what you're capable of.

JOSEFA. You know very little about justice—and nothing about love.

SEVIGNE. (*Crosses* L.) Well—perhaps I'll learn from you—as Ostos did.

JOSEFA. (*Wounded.*) Oh! (*Rises. She flings the handkerchief at him.*) You're heartless!

(SEVIGNE *opens the door, beckons to* ELDERLY GUARD *who enters.* SEVIGNE *hands him the warrant, he glances at it.*)

SEVIGNE. Take her away! (*The* GUARD *puts his hand on her arm, she shakes it off angrily. She turns to look at* SEVIGNE *again. Irritably.*) Oh, get her out of here! (*He avoids looking at her.*)

JOSEFA. (*Quietly, to the* GUARD.) I'm ready.

(*The* GUARD *leads her out, the door closes.* SEVIGNE *sinks wearily into his chair at* C.)

MORESTAN. Very good. Extremely well handled. The fact is, I thought you were about to get your confession, and if you had pressed that final accusation a bit harder—
SEVIGNE. (*He has raised his head slowly.*) Don't be an ass!
MORESTAN. (*Startled.*) What?
SEVIGNE. She's innocent.
MORESTAN. (*Floundering.*) Innocent? Surely not—the evidence—the file—the way you questioned her—
SEVIGNE. I hammered her to show her the danger she was in. If she talks long enough—the idiot!—she'll chatter herself right up the steps to the guillotine.
MORESTAN. Innocent! (*Shrugs helplessly.*) Maybe, but where does that leave *us?*
SEVIGNE. (*Angrily.*) It leaves us with a nice, juicy, *un*solved murder.
MORESTAN. (*Pained.*) The Chief Prosecutor *hates* those! (*Almost pleadingly.*) You're quite sure she's innocent? What I mean to say is, if we have to give somebody the benefit of the doubt, let's give it to the Chief Prosecutor.
SEVIGNE. Come on, let's lock up. For my first day, I've had about enough. (*He starts to gather up the precious lawbooks on his desk, looking at the bulky volume in his hand.*)
MORESTAN. A Magistrate—reading lawbooks all day. I knew this would happen. (*He puts on shoes as:*)

THE CURTAIN FALLS

ACT TWO

THE SCENE: *The same as Act I.*
THE TIME: *A bright, sunny winter afternoon, two days later.*
AT RISE: MORESTAN *is alone in the chamber, at desk,* L., *hard at work transcribing various documents and bits of testimony. He works with an air of disapproval. The door opens slowly, rather timidly, and in the same fashion,* ANTOINETTE SEVIGNE *enters from* U. C.

ANTOINETTE. (*At* C.; *timidly.*) Hello. Am I disturbing you?
MORESTAN. (*Half rises.*) No—not a bit. Come on in. (*She is looking around for the missing member.*) He won't be long. He's with the Chief Prosecutor.
ANTOINETTE. (*Apprehensively.*) The Chief Prosecutor? (*And then.*) Was—it because of the newspapers?
MORESTAN. Probably.
ANTOINETTE. But it wasn't Paul's fault. He was only doing his duty!
MORESTAN. No more, no less. Your husband is absolutely fair and fearless; passionately concerned with the administration of justice. Those are wonderful qualities! (*With a sigh.*) If only he weren't a magistrate!
ANTOINETTE. Is the Chief—difficult?
MORESTAN. When the Chief was on the Bench he was known as Judge Necessity—Judge Necessity—get it? (ANTOINETTE *looks puzzled, he adds gleefully.*) Because necessity knows no law!
ANTOINETTE. (*Dutifully.*) Oh! Oh! that's a good one. (*A hollow tinkle of laughter.*)
MORESTAN. (*Glances at his watch.*) Excuse me. I'll go on with my work. We take up the investigation in a little while.
ANTOINETTE. Yes, I know. Go right ahead. (MORE-

STAN *resumes his copying or transcribing.* ANTOINETTE *fidgets around the office a bit, picking up a text or magazine, putting it down again.* MORESTAN, *meanwhile, rises, crosses behind him to get paper, returns and* ANTOINETTE *of course takes the opportunity to pick up the conversation. Quite artlessly.*) What is she like?

MORESTAN. She? (*And then.*) Oh—she. (*He shrugs, baffled.*)

ANTOINETTE. Is she pretty?

MORESTAN. Yes. (*Sits.*)

ANTOINETTE. The photograph in the paper this morning didn't look very pretty.

MORESTAN. She is. Not at first sight, but later one is aware of it.

ANTOINETTE. Do *you* think she's innocent?

MORESTAN. She says she is.

ANTOINETTE. But don't they all say that?

MORESTAN. (*Thoughtfully.*) She says it differently.

ANTOINETTE. (*Behind desk,* R.; *an outburst.*) It's not fair! We've just arrived, we haven't even found an apartment. Why couldn't Paul get something nice, a white-collar case, like a bank robbery—why should he have *this?* (*Furiously.*) And what right has she got to be innocent?

MORESTAN. (*Vaguely.*) Who knows? The criminal mind—

ANTOINETTE. (*Nervously.*) And Paul is always for the underdog. It's a compulsion. Even if there isn't any underdog, he finds a dog and *puts* him under.

(*She subsides, sits* U. L. *at stove, glancing at some ancient magazines, and in a moment* SEVIGNE *enters. He doesn't instantly see his wife.*)

SEVIGNE. (*Crosses in from* U. C. *to* L. *desk.*) Ah, Morestan, you should have heard the old boy. Really remarkable lung-power for a man of his years— (*And then.*) Antoinette! What a nice surprise! (*Crosses* R. *to her.*)

ANTOINETTE. (BOTH *at* C.) What happened, Paul?

SEVIGNE. (*Crosses* L.) Well—the Chief began with a ringing affirmation of the great guiding principle of the Court: equal justice under law. And then he closed by swearing he'd kick my ass all the way back to Lyons.

ANTOINETTE. Paul!

SEVIGNE. He was joking, of course. (*Without conviction.*) The Chief has a fantastic sense of humor, hasn't he, Morestan? (*Crosses* D. L. *behind* MORESTAN.)

MORESTAN. Fantastic.

ANTOINETTE. (*Crosses Down.*) It's inconvenient, isn't it, that you think the girl is innocent?

SEVIGNE. Yes, very— (*With a mirthless laugh.*) for any number of people, apparently. One funny chattering idiot of a girl and so much money and influence pushing her into a quiet, cozy little cell. (*Wistfully.*) Did you know that Benjamin Beaurevers has three Rolls-Royces? (*Crosses* U. C.; *thoughtfully.*) I have one Simca, vintage 1953, and Josefa Lantenay has only a second-hand bicycle. On sheer horse-power we are definitely out-classed.

ANTOINETTE. (*Outraged.*) We? (*And again.*) *We?* That's *us*—you and I!

SEVIGNE. I'm not forgetting that.

MORESTAN. (*Half-rises; embarrassed.*) Er—perhaps I ought to see about the—er—witness—

SEVIGNE. Sit down, Morestan. (*To* ANTOINETTE.) What do you think I should do? (*Crossing* R.)

ANTOINETTE. (*Confused, angry.*) I don't know. But if your superiors want something done a certain way, then it's your responsibility, isn't it?

SEVIGNE. Up to a point—yes.

ANTOINETTE. Then do it! (*At his helpless gesture.*) It's nothing but sheer ego to defy them. You're jeopardizing your career and everything we've worked for.

SEVIGNE. (*Both at* D. C.) Antoinette— (*Patiently, earnestly.*) I assure you—on my honor and my experience— that I believe the girl is innocent. (*Crosses* R.)

ANTOINETTE. Innocent! A little tramp who doesn't even wear underpants!

SEVIGNE. (*Crosses* L. *to her.*) If she were charged with that I wouldn't lift a finger to help her. But she's accused of murder. I have to care about that. Not about her—*it*. Justice.

ANTOINETTE. That's pompous and pretentious.

SEVIGNE. Is it? (*Crosses* R.; *thoughtfully.*) Yes, I suppose it is. It shouldn't be. I'm a lawyer—and a magistrate—surely I ought to be able to say the word "justice" without sounding like a stuffed shirt.

ANTOINETTE. (*Softer now.*) Oh, Paul, you're such a schoolboy. You can be hoodwinked into anything.

SEVIGNE. (*Gently.*) You ought to know. (*Taking her in his arms.*)

ANTOINETTE. Will you stop this nonsense about the girl?

SEVIGNE. It's too late, I'm afraid. (*And at her sigh, crosses to her.*) I'm sorry. I tried to warn you. Remember? Even before we were married, I told you I was a man of integrity—and you seemed pleased.

ANTOINETTE. (*Ruefully.*) I thought you were lying. (*As he laughs, continues ruefully.*) A lawyer—I never dreamed you were telling the truth.

SEVIGNE. We're tricky. (*Kisses her lightly.*) Now, run along.

ANTOINETTE. All right. (*He has already turned to his table.*) Are you going to question the girl again? (*Crosses* U. C.)

SEVIGNE. We'll start with her.

ANTOINETTE. (*She has picked up her purse and her gloves at* U. R., *drops the gloves on the desk again. Sweetly.*) Goodbye, darling. Get home as soon as you can.

SEVIGNE. I promise.

ANTOINETTE. (*At* U. C.) Goodbye, Monsieur Morestan.

MORESTAN. Goodbye, Madame Sevigne. (*Rises, then sits.*)

SEVIGNE. (*As she is nearly out.*) Antoinette— (*She turns.*) Take your gloves.

ACT II A SHOT IN THE DARK 39

(*He rises, picks them up, hands them to her.* ANTOINETTE *smiles, but she is annoyed.*)

ANTOINETTE. Thank you, darling. It was silly of me to leave them.
SEVIGNE. (*Smiling.*) No, not a bit silly. You wanted an excuse to come back for a look at Josefa Lantenay. (*Giving her a little pat.*) Run along, now.
ANTOINETTE. Really!

(*She sweeps out with as much dignity as she can manage under the circumstances.* SEVIGNE *heaves a sigh, gets back to his desk and the papers.*)

SEVIGNE. (*Crosses* D. R. *behind desk.*) Morestan, when I'm questioning the girl, I shall ask you to bring in another witness—for confrontation.
MORESTAN. Yes—who? (*Rises, crosses* C.)
SEVIGNE. No matter. But when I do, take your time.
MORESTAN. Eh?
SEVIGNE. Fiddle with papers, tie a shoelace—anything, but *take your time.*
MORESTAN. (*Plaintively.*) Indefinitely?
SEVIGNE. (*Crosses* U. R. *behind desk.*) A few moments —you'll be able to judge it for yourself. (*Glancing at his watch.*) See if she's here. Bring her in. (MORESTAN *goes to the door, beckons.* JOSEFA *enters. She is pale, wears no make-up, her hair is dishevelled, she looks ravishing. She seems very subdued, glances at* SEVIGNE *on her entrance, then avoids his eyes.*) Sit down, Mademoiselle.
JOSEFA. (*She shuffles to the indicated chair, is about to sit.*) Mademoiselle! (*She looks at* SEVIGNE *suspiciously.*) You called me: "Mademoiselle." One of your tricks?
SEVIGNE. (*Smiling.*) Sit down, Mademoiselle.
JOSEFA. (*Seated.*) I don't think anyone ever called me that. It's always: "Hey, you!" or just: "Hurry, Josefa!" or: "Be careful with that broom, stupid!"—but never: Mademoiselle. To get that, I had to go to prison first. (*Grudgingly, to* SEVIGNE.) But, thanks, anyway.

SEVIGNE. You're welcome. Now, then, to resume, I would like to— (*Sits.*)

JOSEFA. Oh, that prison! (*Shivers, then accusingly.*) Do you know what it's like?

SEVIGNE. (*Patiently.*) If you'll just listen—

JOSEFA. How would you like it if two dirty old women stripped *you* to the skin, and searched you—everywhere —horribly?

SEVIGNE. Prison is supposed to be unpleasant. (*Pointedly.*) So people will try to avoid being put in it. Now, will you please listen—?

JOSEFA. And this picture they took of me! (*Fishes a newspaper clipping from her pocket.*) Look at that—I look terrible!

SEVIGNE. (*Angrily.*) How did you get that? Prisoners aren't allowed newspapers.

JOSEFA. Ha! A lot you know. In a women's prison, the first few days, you can get anything. The other girls buzz around you, offering you extra food, candy, newspapers —oh, you pay, don't worry, and tonight or tomorrow night they'll be coming around to me— (*With a gesture of disgust.*) Your prison!

SEVIGNE. It is not my prison. And stop babbling.

JOSEFA. All right. I'll be good. Just don't put me back in that horrible hole. I'll do anything. I'll confess, if you'll let me go.

SEVIGNE. Shut up—and *listen!*

JOSEFA. Yes, sir. (*She winces as she sees him take the file. As he turns back to her she takes off her coat, folds it carefully over the back of her chair. She sits down again, giving* SEVIGNE *a smile.*) What do you want me to tell you?

SEVIGNE. (*Briskly.*) We have some unfinished business, you and I—now, then: the name of your lover? (*Crosses behind desk, sits.*)

JOSEFA. (*Promptly.*) Miguel Ostos. (*And at* SEVIGNE'S *stern look, plaintively.*) Well, he *was*—

SEVIGNE. The *other* man.

ACT II   A SHOT IN THE DARK   41

JOSEFA. (*Pained.*) He left town weeks ago—and, really, he's got nothing to do with all this—

SEVIGNE. (*Severely.*) I'm not surprised that Ostos beat you.

JOSEFA. I know. Even Miguel said he did it only in self-defense, when I was being too much of an idiot.

SEVIGNE. (*Sternly.*) Do you want to go back to prison?

JOSEFA. (*Meekly.*) No—I'd rather you beat me.

SEVIGNE. I'll ask you just once more, and I warn you—

(*He stops short as the door opens and* ANTOINETTE *enters, coolly, quite poised, at* U. C.)

ANTOINETTE. (*Brazenly.*) Oh, darling, forgive me—I forgot my gloves.

SEVIGNE. (*Rises.*) WHAT?

(MORESTAN *leans way over his writing to conceal his amusement.*)

ANTOINETTE. I must have left them on a chair, or on your desk— (*Looks for them, but plainly with her eyes riveted on* JOSEFA. JOSEFA, *embarrassed, pulls her skirt down as far as it will go, apparently the only gesture of modesty she knows.*)

SEVIGNE. Antoinette! Will you kindly leave us— (*Sternly.*) at once!

ANTOINETTE. Ah, here they are! (*Pretending to take them from under a book on the desk. Crosses to* C.)

SEVIGNE. (*Seething.*) All right—now go! (ANTOINETTE *is pulling the gloves on, finger by finger, studying* JOSEFA.) Antoinette!

ANTOINETTE. Yes, darling. Just going. (*Ominously.*) Get home as early as you can—we have a lot to talk about. (*She goes, slamming the door.*)

(SEVIGNE *sits.*)

JOSEFA. (*Curiously.*) Your wife? (SEVIGNE, *still seeth-*

ing, ignores her, getting himself in hand again for the interrogation.) You married a young one, eh? (*In a tone of respect.*) It's funny—I didn't think you were the type.

SEVIGNE. Are there any other comments you want to make about my wife?

JOSEFA. (*Unenthusiastically.*) She's very pretty.

SEVIGNE. Thanks. (*Drily.*) She liked you, too. (JOSEFA *mugs. Braces herself as he opens the file.*) Now, then— the name of the man? (*As she stares back at him.*) Ah, you're being your sweet, reasonable self again, eh?

JOSEFA. (*With spirit.*) I want to be. I cried for eleven hours in that filthy cell. The other women said it was a new record for the prison. And if you send me back, it will be worse—

SEVIGNE. So?

JOSEFA. I *won't* give you the name of someone innocent—and let you get him mixed up in this—I call that being an informer.

SEVIGNE. I guarantee you that in a few minutes you'll give me the name.

JOSEFA. All right. I don't mind waiting— (SEVIGNE *rises. At the look in his eye.*) That's right. Go on—hit me!

SEVIGNE. How did you get on with your employer?

JOSEFA. (*Enthusiastically.*) Madame Beaurevers? She's marvellous. We're all crazy about her. She's been more like a wonderful older sister than an employer to me.

SEVIGNE. When Inspector Colas asked you about Madame, you said . . . (*From the file.*) "She's all right—if you like the snooty, ice-box type!"

JOSEFA. (*Shocked.*) *I* said that? About Madame? (*Conscience-stricken, emphatically.*) I'm an ungrateful pig.

SEVIGNE. And Monsieur Beaurevers?

JOSEFA. Well . . . (*Her gesture is a "comme-ci, comma-ca" indication.*) He's very elegant, you know. (*With a hint of care in her responses.*) He's probably very nice, too, but quite honestly, I never really understood most of what he was saying.

SEVIGNE. (*Sits.*) Did you have *many* conversations?

JOSEFA. Well, as a parlormaid, in *his* parlor—naturally, he had to tell me things. Don't you talk to *your* parlormaid?

SEVIGNE. I will, when I have one. So you didn't get along with Monsieur Beaurevers?

JOSEFA. Well, I wouldn't say that. But you see what I am—a simple girl, and I talk too much—and Monsieur Beaurevers is a banker, from a noble family, really terrifically well-bred.

SEVIGNE. In other words, there was a gulf between you?

JOSEFA. That's right—a real gulf.

SEVIGNE. Were you and Ostos on vacation together?

JOSEFA. No. Miguel went to the Basque country because there were great bull-fights in Dax, Bayonne, Biarritz—all over. Dominguin and Ordonnez! Mano a mano! He couldn't miss those! (*Sadly.*) Poor Miguel!

SEVIGNE. And you?

JOSEFA. Oh, I stayed with the family, at their country house. So near home for me. I could be with my old papa.

SEVIGNE. In October, you were all back in Paris. And Ostos' day off was changed?

JOSEFA. Oh? Was that when that happened?

SEVIGNE. Yes. And Miguel Ostos began raving about his jealousy.

JOSEFA. (*Carefully.*) You ought to remember, he was always raving about *something*. If it wasn't me, it was the Paris weather, or French food, or cowardly bulls—he never just talked, he raved.

SEVIGNE. (*From the file.*) Police interrogation of the cook: "A week after we came back to Paris, in October, Miguel said that Josefa had turned against him. 'I was a fool to let her go to the country alone,' he cried. 'She's been tripping over roots again down there, and without *me*.'" (*Glances at* JOSEFA *for comment.*)

JOSEFA. That cook—still giving me heartburn!

SEVIGNE. What happened at Hauterive in September?

JOSEFA. (*Carefully.*) Well, it rained part of the time—

I saw quite a lot of Papa— (*Glances up at him to see how she's doing.*) had picnics and went swimming with some of the boys and girls I knew from the old days— that sort of thing, nothing much.

SEVIGNE. Did you enjoy your holiday?

JOSEFA. M-m-m-m—it was nice. Dull, but nice. (*She looks up at him, searching for some clue to this line of questioning. He is blank.*) Why are you so interested in my vacation?

SEVIGNE. I'm not, really. Just passing the time. (*Casually.*) Morestan, show in the witness Benjamin Beaurevers.

(JOSEFA *comes straight up in her chair excitedly.* MORESTAN, *following orders, putters about on his desk.*)

JOSEFA. Monsieur Beaurevers—he is *here?*

SEVIGNE. (*Ignoring her.*) Hurry, Morestan!

MORESTAN. I'm hurrying. (*Ties shoe in* C.)

JOSEFA. The way I look! They took everything away from me in prison—powder, lipstick, *everything.* (*Crosses* R. *to window, bites her lips to give them color, smooths her hair, looks in the window in lieu of a mirror, fixing herself up as best she can.*) Oh, why does he have to see me looking like this? (MORESTAN *has gone to the door,* SEVIGNE *is looking at* JOSEFA *gravely, and she is suddenly aware of what she has betrayed.*) Oh! (*She turns from the window slowly, facing him, sinks into window seat.*)

SEVIGNE. Remember—I said you would give me the name of the man?

(MORESTAN *crosses* U. C.)

JOSEFA. (*Sadly, coldly.*) Are you happy doing this kind of work, Monsieur?

SEVIGNE. (*Ironically.*) Try not to hate me too much.

JOSEFA. I've never hated anyone. And I don't hate you. But don't be surprised if you hate yourself.

SEVIGNE. (*Rises; roughly.*) Idiot! Must you be tricked into helping yourself?

JOSEFA. (*Rises.*) Idiot? Because I won't betray someone? Thank you!

SEVIGNE. All right, Joan of Arc—sit down.

(JOSEFA *sits. At the door,* MADAME BEAUREVERS *is pushing past* MORESTAN, *who is trying to keep her out.*)

MORESTAN. Your interrogation is *later,* Madame.

(MME. BEAUREVERS *crosses in to* R. *desk.* MORESTAN *follows. She walks past.*)

MADAME BEAUREVERS. Not at all. You've misunderstood. (*She is very beautiful, chic, and carries the situation with an air of great gaiety.*)

MORESTAN. No, Madame, there is no mistake. Please wait.

(BENJAMIN BEAUREVERS *has followed his wife into the chamber. He is supremely elegant, quite handsome, very sure of himself. He makes no effort whatever to conform to any surroundings that are foreign to him.* MADAME BEAUREVERS *is instantly intent on charming* SEVIGNE, *extending her hand.*)

MADAME BEAUREVERS. My dear Judge, I was just explaining to your clerk—

(MORESTAN *crosses* R. *behind desk;* BEAUREVERS *crosses to* C.)

SEVIGNE. I'm not a judge, Madame—only a magistrate. Will you be kind enough—

MADAME BEAUREVERS. (*Interrupting him.*) Charming! What a cozy little office you have here! (*Glancing around the shabby interior.*) Strange, isn't it—I feel quite at home here. Perhaps because so many friends and relatives are in the judiciary.

SEVIGNE. Thank you, Madame. If you will be kind enough to wait in the corridor—

MADAME BEAUREVERS. (*One word at a time.*) Wait? In—the—corridor?

SEVIGNE. Or, if you prefer, in that adjoining room— (*Indicating the door at* L.)

MADAME BEAUREVERS. But surely, you wouldn't think of questioning my husband alone—without me?

SEVIGNE. In my opinion, Madame, that would be best.

MADAME BEAUREVERS. Ridiculous! Why can't I be present?

SEVIGNE. Because in this office, Madame, it is I who gives orders, and with all due respect, I must ask you to wait outside.

(JOSEFA *is all smiles at the way he is handling* MADAME BEAUREVERS.)

MADAME BEAUREVERS. (*Ominously.*) Benjamin, did you hear that?

BEAUREVERS. I did, my dear Dominique.

MADAME BEAUREVERS. Is that all you have to say?

BEAUREVERS. No doubt our learned friend could have expressed himself with more affability but he may perhaps be pressed for time.

JOSEFA. (*Rises; aside, to* SEVIGNE.) Fantastic, isn't it? I never understand half of what he says.

MADAME BEAUREVERS. (*Turning to* JOSEFA.) And we have you to thank, Josefa, for all this unpleasantness.

JOSEFA. (*Indifferently.*) So it seems, Madame.

MADAME BEAUREVERS. And to think I have always had such confidence in you! And I was kind to you!

JOSEFA. Very kind, Madame.

SEVIGNE. Morestan, please show Madame Beaurevers to the corridor—at once.

(MORESTAN *crosses to* U. C.)

MADAME BEAUREVERS. (*Ominously.*) Benjamin!
BEAUREVERS. Yes, my dear Dominique?
MADAME BEAUREVERS. Do you hear the tone of voice in which this man speaks to me?
BEAUREVERS. I detected no coarseness or undue lack of courtesy in his address, my dear.
MADAME BEAUREVERS. (*Resignedly, furiously.*) Very well, I'll wait.
SEVIGNE. Thank you, Madame.

(MADAME BEAUREVERS *exits* U. C., *slamming the door.* MORESTAN *returns to his place at* L.)

BEAUREVERS. (*Crosses* R. *a step.*) I must explain to you, my dear Judge, that Dominique—Madame Beaurevers—does not mean to be overbearing, but hers is an ancient family, descended, I believe, in a direct line from Attila the Hun.
SEVIGNE. Please sit down.
BEAUREVERS. Thank you, my dear Judge.

(BEAUREVERS *sits* C. JOSEFA *goes to* U. L., *sits; pulls in* C.)

SEVIGNE. I am not a Judge—only a Magistrate. (*Glances at* MORESTAN *to see if he is ready, then to* BEAUREVERS.) Your full name, please, address and profession.
BEAUREVERS. Benjamin Beaurevers, 112 rue de la Faisanderie, banker.
JOSEFA. (*Solicitously.*) You've lost weight, Monsieur.
BEAUREVERS. A little. And you don't look too well, my poor Josefa.
JOSEFA. Oh, well, the prison—you know—they don't let us have make-up.
BEAUREVERS. Prison! Poor Josefa!
JOSEFA. (*Pulls chair closer.*) Oh, don't worry about me. You know I can look after myself—

(SEVIGNE *has been tapping, louder and louder, with a*

pencil. It finally communicates itself to both BEAUREVERS *and* JOSEFA, *who look at him.*)

SEVIGNE. (*Apologetically.*) Thank you. It's rude of me to interrupt, but we have this murder on our hands—

BEAUREVERS. (*Heartily.*) Of course. (*And to* JOSEFA.) Pay attention, Josefa.

JOSEFA. (*Meekly.*) Yes, sir. (*Then sotto voce, indicating Sevigne.*) Don't worry—he's nice. (*Waggles her finger chummily at* SEVIGNE, *who is stupefied by this intimacy. She goes on whispering to* BEAUREVERS.) At first I didn't think so, and he *did* send me to prison, but he's really very nice.

SEVIGNE. Be quiet!

JOSEFA. (*Amiably.*) Yes, sir.

SEVIGNE. (*To* BEAUREVERS.) Now, then, after you had returned to Paris in October, why was Ostos' day off changed from Wednesday to Thursday?

BEAUREVERS. (*Carelessly.*) I suppose it was due to some idiosyncrasy of household management.

SEVIGNE. Would you mind using simpler language in your replies?

BEAUREVERS. I wouldn't mind, but I don't know how.

SEVIGNE. Did you personally order the change?

BEAUREVERS. No. (*Adding.*) Is that simple enough?

SEVIGNE. Did you know that Miguel Ostos had been the lover of Josefa Lantenay?

BEAUREVERS. I share the philosophy of the late Emperor Frederick the Great: "In my State," declared His Majesty, "every man shall amuse himself as he sees fit."

SEVIGNE. Furthermore, that in addition to Ostos, there was another man?

BEAUREVERS. Ah, youth, youth!

SEVIGNE. Did you know the identity of the other man?

BEAUREVERS. Without infringing on the rights and privileges of your high office, may *I* ask a question?

SEVIGNE. (*Nodding.*) Please.

BEAUREVERS. Do *you* know the identity of the other man?

ACT II   A SHOT IN THE DARK   49

SEVIGNE. I think so—yes.

BEAUREVERS. Ah!— (*Then, carefully.*) I feel a natural apprehension about my wife, you understand—do you suppose we can continue to share the secret between us?

SEVIGNE. I hope so.

JOSEFA. I swear I told him nothing. But my idiot face betrayed me when you were announced.

SEVIGNE. Then you admit that you are the man?

BEAUREVERS. I do, and with pleasure.

JOSEFA. (*Happily.*) Thank you for saying that. And simply, so I could understand it.

SEVIGNE. (*To* BEAUREVERS.) Do you know how to shut her up?

BEAUREVERS. Frankly, not for very long—and that only by a method I should hesitate to employ before witnesses of either sex.

SEVIGNE. Where did your affair begin—and when?

BEAUREVERS. At our country house, in Hauterive, in September.

JOSEFA. (*Promptly.*) Thursday, 11th September, just after twelve noon.

BEAUREVERS. Yes, I remember that I was starting to think about lunch.

SEVIGNE. (*Drily.*) And something put it out of your mind?

BEAUREVERS. Man cannot live by bread alone.

SEVIGNE. It was sudden, was it?

BEAUREVERS. To say that I had been for some time becoming aware of Josefa would not be entirely untruthful.

SEVIGNE. (*Puzzled.*) Are you answering: "Yes" or "No"?

BEAUREVERS. I am answering—the rest is up to you.

SEVIGNE. All right. Now then, back to your country house, September 11th, just before lunch. Will you kindly take it from there?

BEAUREVERS. The country, in September, is not quite the liveliest atmosphere in France, you understand. My wife has her horses, and friends who ride and hunt, but strange as it may seem to you, I am not the outdoor type.

SEVIGNE. (*Drily.*) I accept that.

BEAUREVERS. The indoor life, in fact, often yields rather more adventure.

SEVIGNE. I know. That's why we're all here.

JOSEFA. (*To* BEAUREVERS.) He doesn't like it when you keep on straying from the point.

BEAUREVERS. Oh. My apologies. (*Groping for the main thread of the enquiry.*) Er—where were we?

JOSEFA. (*Gently prodding his memory.*) The library at Hauterive—I was waxing the floor—remember?

BEAUREVERS. (*Beaming.*) Ah, yes. How could I forget? (*To* SEVIGNE.) A superb room. Almost fifty feet in length and thirty across. Josefa is an excellent worker, you know, and she had the floor gleaming like a skating rink. Unfortunately—or fortunately—depending on the point of view—soon after I entered, she tripped—

SEVIGNE. And fell?

BEAUREVERS. (*Surprised.*) Just so.

SEVIGNE. You jumped forward to help her, and then you *both* fell?

BEAUREVERS. But, my dear chap, that's precisely what happened! How did you know?

SEVIGNE. Statistics. Continue.

BEAUREVERS. (*Delicately.*) Well, there we were, slipping and sliding—to be entirely truthful, I must tell you that she wears very little in the way of—

JOSEFA. (*Cheerfully.*) Oh, he knows that.

BEAUREVERS. (*Taken aback.*) Oh! (*Respectfully, to* SEVIGNE.) I must say that your examinations are extremely thorough.

SEVIGNE. And that is when Josefa Lantenay became your mistress?

BEAUREVERS. (*Astounded.*) My *what?*

JOSEFA. (*Gently.*) He means *me.*

BEAUREVERS. (*Honestly surprised.*) But of course! You *are* my mistress! (*Apologetically, to both.*) I had never thought of it in precisely that way. (*To* SEVIGNE.) Semantically, of course, you are entirely correct.

SEVIGNE. Semantically, biologically, legally, that is the fact, isn't it?

BEAUREVERS. (*Emphatically.*) Oh, yes!

SEVIGNE. And from then on?

BEAUREVERS. I had not intended to embark on a prolonged relationship— (*To* JOSEFA.) I mean no offense, my dear.

JOSEFA. I didn't even know you were talking about *me*.

BEAUREVERS. (*To* SEVIGNE.) But—as I had already implied—Hauterive in September offers only limited and monotonous amusements, and Josefa— (*A sigh of memory.*) My learned friend, this girl is more attractive than you would think possible!

SEVIGNE. And Ostos?

BEAUREVERS. (*Judicially.*) Not nearly as attractive. (*With a tolerant shrug.*) Of course, if your taste runs to sullen Spanish chauffeurs—

SEVIGNE. I meant, how did Ostos react?

JOSEFA. Miguel knew nothing.

BEAUREVERS. He was on vacation in the Basque country. An *aficionado*. He had the Spanish passion for bullfights.

JOSEFA. (*Beaming.*) Olé—Olé!

BEAUREVERS. (*Indulgently.*) Precisely. Olé! Olé!

(*They look at each other very fondly, lost to their surroundings.* SEVIGNE *draws them back by tapping sharply with his pencil.*)

SEVIGNE. Now, when you returned to Paris in October, what about Ostos *then?*

BEAUREVERS. As you have surmised, my learned friend, it was found expedient to change his free day. On other occasions it was relatively simple to find or invent an errand for him in some remote part of the city. Even in the suburbs. (*Enjoying the memory.*) Once when I was coming back from the South, he waited all night long at

Orly Field for my plane. Actually, I arrived at dinnertime—at Le Bourget—and came home quietly by taxi.— (*Smiling at* JOSEFA.) Remember?

JOSEFA. (*Tenderly.*) M-m-m-m-m! (*And then.*) Miguel caught cold waiting and he cursed and sneezed for two days.

BEAUREVERS. It was marvellous being with Josefa, while he waited all night at the wrong airport.

JOSEFA. (*Cautiously, to* SEVIGNE.) It was the idea of the joke, you understand—there was no real anger between Monsieur Beaurevers and Miguel—

BEAUREVERS. Nonsense—I detested him.

SEVIGNE. Before your affair with Josefa—or since?

BEAUREVERS. Oh, long before. For one thing, he was well over six feet, and I usually take an instant dislike to anyone taller than I am. (*Amending it.*) Naturally, that's not true of General De Gaulle.

SEVIGNE. Your dislike of Ostos was based entirely on altitude?

BEAUREVERS. (*Thoughtfully.*) No. It's true that he was a tall, handsome brute, and looked very well in uniform, but there was also a baffling air of insolence about him. He seemed to resent being ordered to do this or that.

JOSEFA. That's true. It was his pride. He complained bitterly. "Just because I'm a chauffeur and a valet," he said, "they treat me like a servant."

SEVIGNE. (*To* BEAUREVERS.) Why did you keep him in your employ?

BEAUREVERS. (*Shrugs.*) At first because he was a skilled chauffeur—and then, afterwards, I was afraid that if I sent him packing, he might take Josefa with him.

JOSEFA. Ah, that was kind. Thank you.

BEAUREVERS. Not at all. (*And to* SEVIGNE.) In any event, the problem of Ostos no longer exists.

SEVIGNE. Yes, that's certainly true, isn't it? (*Almost with admiration.*) Couldn't be better if you had arranged it yourself, could it?

BEAUREVERS. (*Unruffled.*) If you are speaking as a

member of the staff of the Prosecutor, it would perhaps be best if I made no comment.

SEVIGNE. Why was a gun kept in the glove compartment of the Rolls-Royce?

BEAUREVERS. (*Innocently.*) Which Rolls-Royce?

SEVIGNE. (*Resigned.*) I let myself in for that, didn't I? All right, the limousine. (*And as* BEAUREVERS *shrugs.*) *Don't* tell me it was standard equipment.

BEAUREVERS. The vehicle in question is actually owned by our bank. (*Delicately.*) Some aspect of taxation is involved. It is sometimes used for inconspicuous transfers of large sums—valuables.

SEVIGNE. In any event, you knew it was there?

BEAUREVERS. I *put* it there.

SEVIGNE. And you're familiar with ordinary fire-arms?

BEAUREVERS. My dear fellow, I was one of the best shots in France.

JOSEFA. He gave it up. He's too kind to kill anything. (*Helping all she can.*) And he won't admit it, but now his eyesight is terrible.

SEVIGNE. If Monsieur Beaurevers wants a lawyer, why don't you let him choose one? (*And back to* BEAUREVERS.) You were the first in the room after Ostos was shot?

BEAUREVERS. Yes—that is so.

SEVIGNE. You hesitate?

BEAUREVERS. Only because I believe it is a question of some importance. (*Firmly.*) I was the first.

SEVIGNE. You were attracted to the scene by the shot?

BEAUREVERS. Yes. I was in my dressing-room. At first I thought it might have been the back-fire from a car, but in our street, cars don't do that. So—I rushed downstairs to investigate.

SEVIGNE. On entering the room, what did you see?

BEAUREVERS. Josefa was lying at the foot of the bed . . .

SEVIGNE. (*As he hesitates.*) Yes, go on.

BEAUREVERS. She was nude—

SEVIGNE. Yes, that fact has been established by *all* the witnesses.

(JOSEFA *tugs at her skirt.*)

BEAUREVERS. My immediate concern, of course, was for Josefa, but I saw at once that she was unharmed. Her chest was rising and falling regularly, in a manner both tranquil and profound—rising and falling— (*His voice becomes quite bemused with the memory.*)

SEVIGNE. (*Drily.*) You didn't also happen to notice the body of Miguel Ostos anywhere in the room?

BEAUREVERS. (*Recalled.*) Oh, yes. (*Matter of fact.*) He was lying just inside the door. I had to step over him, in fact, to get to Josefa. (*Adding.*) Which I did.

SEVIGNE. Ostos was still alive, was he not?

BEAUREVERS. He was.

SEVIGNE. He was quite conscious?

BEAUREVERS. Well, he was alive—gasping—

SEVIGNE. He was trying to speak—to say something?

BEAUREVERS. (*Reluctantly.*) I had that impression, yes.

SEVIGNE. (*Patiently, digging.*) Could you clearly understand what he was trying to say?

BEAUREVERS. Well, you know, a foreigner, under the best conditions his accent was quite coarse, not at all Parisian— (*As if this were quite painful to him.*) Also, he was a type who spoke wildly at all times, even when he had *not* been shot.

SEVIGNE. (*Flatly.*) What were his exact words?

BEAUREVERS. (*Reproachfully.*) A dying man—and you quibble about exact words?

SEVIGNE. (*Patiently.*) *Approximately* what were his exact words?

(BEAUREVERS *looks pained, and* JOSEFA *leaps into the breach.*)

JOSEFA. It's unfair to ask Monsieur Beaurevers that question in front of me.

BEAUREVERS. Thank you for understanding, Josefa. (*To* SEVIGNE.) Sensitive. It's quite amazing, really. She's had little or no education.

SEVIGNE. What did Ostos say? I must insist that you answer.

JOSEFA. *I'll* answer. Miguel said: "Josefa, why did you do it?" He said it over and over again.

SEVIGNE. Why do *you* answer? Did you hear the words spoken?

JOSEFA. I was unconscious. I'm repeating what you told me.

SEVIGNE. (*Mildly.*) And I am repeating what Monsieur Beaurevers told the police. (*At* BEAUREVERS' *pained look.*) That's true, isn't it?

BEAUREVERS. (*Reluctantly.*) Yes. Actually, it was my wife who mentioned it to Inspector Colas—

SEVIGNE. (*Pressing the point.*) But it was you who heard Ostos say it? (*Indicating* JOSEFA.) It remains the principal cause of her incrimination.

JOSEFA. (*Defending* BEAUREVERS.) Nonsense! What about the gun in my hand? (*Comfortingly, to* BEAUREVERS.) Pay no attention, Monsieur Beaurevers—there is plenty of evidence against me.

BEAUREVERS. (*To* SEVIGNE.) I have the impression that you are reproaching me for aiding justice in this affair.

JOSEFA. Very good. (*Unaware of her own peril, or ignoring it; to* SEVIGNE.) What do you say to that?

SEVIGNE. (*To* BEAUREVERS.) I was merely surprised that you could so blithely incriminate a girl who has meant something to you.

BEAUREVERS. It was not something that I enjoyed doing, you understand—

SEVIGNE. At any rate, your statement to the police incriminates her on the unverifiable words of a dead man.

BEAUREVERS. I am not entirely sure that I like the implications of the word "unverifiable." Are you making the point that I invented these words?

SEVIGNE. Well, it is possible that you *might have* invented them.

JOSEFA. (*Indignant.*) Oh! (*To* BEAUREVERS.) Don't let him say such wicked things. Tell him who you are!

BEAUREVERS. It takes so long.

SEVIGNE. (*Sternly.*) The point at issue is the statement allegedly made by a dying man. In a murder case, that is crucial.

BEAUREVERS. Why? If I were dying, I might say anything.

SEVIGNE. In a less sophisticated environment, the assumption is that in these circumstances one tells the truth. (*And then, angrily.*) Damn it! You've got me talking that way!

BEAUREVERS. (*Courteously.*) I am honored.

SEVIGNE. (*Angrily.*) I'm not. Bluntly, then, you were the first person in the room after Ostos was shot. The girl is unconscious, Ostos is dying. You are alone. You have the opportunity to put into Ostos' mouth words that seem useful.

JOSEFA. That's the silliest thing I ever heard!

SEVIGNE. (*Ominously.*) Oh, is it?

JOSEFA. Yes, it is. Words like: "Josefa, why did you do it?" If Monsieur Beaurevers made up that sentence, it would be five times longer and nobody would know what it meant.

BEAUREVERS. A valid point. As you yourself have observed, my speech does have traces of pomposity. And now, if I may comment on your own mode of speech, I am intrigued by your choice of the word "useful." *Why* would I find it useful to invent Ostos' last words?

SEVIGNE. Because for some days before the crime, Ostos suspected you. Furthermore, you knew it.

JOSEFA. He didn't know it. I knew it, but Monsieur Beaurevers did not.

BEAUREVERS. (*Relieved.*) Ah—there you are.

SEVIGNE. (*Rises.*) We'll see. (*Reaches for the file on his desk.* JOSEFA *winces.*)

JOSEFA. (*Whispered, to* BEAUREVERS.) Watch out for

that book—it's loaded! (*At a glare from* SEVIGNE, *she subsides.*)

SEVIGNE. Now, then— (*Rising, crosses Down around desk, addressing* BEAUREVERS *formally.*) I refer to a conversation you had with Madame Marthe Herbeux—

BEAUREVERS. Who?

JOSEFA. The cook—Camel-Face.

SEVIGNE. (*Annoyed, continuing.*) —a few days before the shooting she warned you to stop your affair with Josefa Lantenay. She warned you that Ostos suspected what was going on— (BEAUREVERS *looks at him, impassive.*) and you replied: "What can I do, Marthe? I can't give her up—she's in my blood."

JOSEFA. (*Enchanted.*) Me? In *your* blood? (*Beside herself with joy.*) What an honor!

(BEAUREVERS *is troubled and seeing his concern,* JOSEFA'S *pleasure vanishes. She watches and listens closely.*)

SEVIGNE. Well?

BEAUREVERS. (*Carefully.*) It does not seem to be an entirely characteristic remark for me to make, does it?

SEVIGNE. Are you denying that you made it?

BEAUREVERS. No—it's just that I can't remember.

SEVIGNE. If I read more of that conversation— (*Opening the file.*) perhaps your memory will improve?

BEAUREVERS. You can try, but quite candidly, I doubt it.

(*At* SEVIGNE'S *frown,* JOSEFA *leaps into the breach.*)

JOSEFA. Monsieur Beaurevers has a terrible memory! He forgets dates, names, places—everything.

SEVIGNE. (*To* BEAUREVERS.) Charming, isn't it? The girl is accused of murder, and all she thinks about is how to defend *you.*

BEAUREVERS. Yes, I find it touching and beautiful. Thank you, Josefa.

JOSEFA. (*Embarrassed.*) It's nothing.

BEAUREVERS. No, my dear Josefa, it is something very special which I shall always remember.

(*They are getting lost in each other once more and* SE-VIGNE *taps sharply with his pencil.*)

SEVIGNE. Please, no tripping over roots here— (*And as* BEAUREVERS *turns back to him.*) The cook also told you that Ostos had been brandishing a knife, and you told her not to worry— (*Consulting the file.*) And I quote: "A knife is a romantic but outmoded weapon in terms of modern armament, especially if opposed by a gun."

BEAUREVERS. (*Reluctantly.*) I admit, that *sounds* like me.—

JOSEFA. (*Quickly.*) It's ridiculous—can you imagine Monsieur Beaurevers in that kind of conversation with a cook?

SEVIGNE. (*Crosses* L.; *angrily.*) Shut up!

JOSEFA. (*Carrying on desperately.*) And besides, there were no witnesses.

SEVIGNE. (*Furiously.*) Another word, and I'll throw you out!

BEAUREVERS. (*Calmly.*) Just the same, an excellent point has been made—no witnesses.

SEVIGNE. (*Coldly.*) If it's witnesses you want, then I will refer to your conversation at the Volney Club with Monsieur Guillaume Ancenis. (*He has whipped out some pages of testimony. Crosses* D. R. *behind* BEAUREVERS.) You confided in Monsieur Ancenis that you loved a certain "Jo-Jo." You didn't tell him that your "Jo-Jo" was also your maid, but you did say— (*Brandishing the paper.*) "To keep her I would be capable of anything. Even divorce. *Even a crime.*"

BEAUREVERS. Oh, that son of a bitch! (*He is plainly taken aback.*)

SEVIGNE. Splendid! Your speech is much simpler now! The bartender and two other members have verified this conversation.

BEAUREVERS. (*Bitterly.*) That's club life for you nowadays!

SEVIGNE. Is your memory improving?

BEAUREVERS. (*Reluctantly.*) I remember something like that conversation—

SEVIGNE. Congratulations!

BEAUREVERS. (*Grudgingly.*) Those damn witnesses! (*Steaming.*) A private conversation—*in my club*. And I can't even resign; I bought a life membership!

JOSEFA. (*She is alert to the danger of this testimony. Rises.*) It was nothing but talk—loose talk. He was probably on his seventh whisky—

BEAUREVERS. Josefa! Be still! (JOSEFA *sits. He studies* SEVIGNE *as if measuring the menace.*) Are you implying that I killed Ostos?

SEVIGNE. (*Crosses Down behind desk, sits. Casually, lightly.*) Well, let's see how it shapes up, shall we? A charge of murder, to be sustained, consists of three major elements: Motive, opportunity, premeditation. Your conversations with the cook and at the club provide a motive; opportunity certainly existed; and premeditation may be assumed if you arranged to be alone in the house—

BEAUREVERS. (*Affably.*) What I had in mind was not murder.

SEVIGNE. In addition, you were the first to appear at the scene of the crime—

BEAUREVERS. Please bear in mind: *after* the crime.

SEVIGNE. (*Deliberately.*) True—but if you had arranged matters that way— (*He lets the accusation trail off.*)

JOSEFA. (*Shocked.*) Oh!

BEAUREVERS. (*With great dignity.*) It is just such innuendo and insinuation that make a hollow mockery of justice in our times. (*Rising; crosses* U. C.) I wish you good day.

SEVIGNE. (*Mildly.*) Good day. (*And then.*) I think you'll find that Madame Beaurevers is still waiting in that corridor— (*Indicating the door.* BEAUREVERS *stops, turns, comes back to his chair.*) Thank you.

BEAUREVERS. A man caught between a prosecutor and his wife has little or no choice. (*Facing* SEVIGNE.) Continue.

SEVIGNE. Normally, the cook would have been in the house that night, but you bribed her to go out.

JOSEFA. That cook—with a mouth bigger than her oven—

SEVIGNE. (*Rises; turning on her.*) Oh—*you* again. (*She is intimidated by something in his manner now.*) Do you know the penalty for perjury?

JOSEFA. Perjury?

SEVIGNE. Lying!

JOSEFA. (*Relieved.*) Oh—lying. (*Eagerly, smiling.*) But I don't mean any harm when I do it—

SEVIGNE. (*From the file.*) Josefa Lantenay, in your interrogation two days ago, you were asked the following question: "On the night of the crime, did you have any visitors other than Miguel Ostos?" You evaded the question by jabbering about everything under the sun but when you were finally forced to reply you said: "No!" (*Snaps the file shut with a thump.*) Do you now want to change your answer?

JOSEFA. (*Weakly.*) No.

SEVIGNE. One more chance: Did you have any other visitors?

JOSEFA. (*Rising.*) Send me back to prison!

SEVIGNE. (*Furious.*) Sit down!

JOSEFA. I insist.

BEAUREVERS. (*Quietly.*) Answer the question, Josefa.

JOSEFA. (*Startled.*) What? Oh, no— (*She sinks back into her chair.*)

(*There is a long pause.*)

SEVIGNE. (*Sits.*) It seems to have answered itself—thank you.

BEAUREVERS. We *were* together that night—from eight

o'clock until ten. My wife was visiting friends, it was a simple matter to get rid of the cook for the evening, and Ostos was sent on an errand to our branch bank in Lyons.

SEVIGNE. Yes, that is confirmed by the police.

BEAUREVERS. *I'm* a fast driver, and I could not have been back before midnight, at the earliest. It's utter madness that he was home at eleven. I would have sworn it was impossible.

SEVIGNE. (*Gently.*) I'll bet you were surprised to see him.

BEAUREVERS. Eh? (*Startled momentarily, then he looks thoughtfully at* SEVIGNE.) Ah, yes, I see what you mean. You're suggesting that he found us together.

SEVIGNE. (*Matter of fact.*) A jealous rage—Ostos was famous for those, wasn't he? He attacked you, and you fired in legitimate self-defence.

BEAUREVERS. (*Drily.*) Is that a firm offer?

SEVIGNE. (*In the same tone.*) I can't give it to you in writing.

BEAUREVERS. It won't be necessary. I left Josefa at ten o'clock.

JOSEFA. (*Instantly.*) True. Ten o'clock on the dot. (*As* SEVIGNE *looks at her.*) I heard the clock striking, and I looked at my watch.

SEVIGNE. (*Back to* BEAUREVERS.) Why ten o'clock—since you believed Ostos couldn't be back until after midnight?

BEAUREVERS. Unfortunately, my wife's arrival could not be as accurately predicted. (*Delicately.*) Besides— eight to ten—one is no longer in the first fine flush of youth— (*Turning to* MORESTAN, *who clears his throat.*) My dear fellow, without prejudice to the investigation, you might omit that last remark.

JOSEFA. (*Always the defender.*) Besides, it's not true.

BEAUREVERS. Thank you, Josefa.

SEVIGNE. (*Musing.*) Eight to ten—and well out of the way before anything happened to Ostos. You had another plan to meet that night, didn't you?

JOSEFA. No.

BEAUREVERS. (*Simultaneously.*) Yes.
SEVIGNE. At eleven o'clock? The time Ostos was shot?
JOSEFA. No.
BEAUREVERS. (*Simultaneously.*) Yes.
SEVIGNE. (*Drily.*) Surely, what you had in mind takes two?
BEAUREVERS. We had planned to meet at eleven o'clock. I sent Josefa a note telling her so.
JOSEFA. (*Puzzled, makes another outburst.*) No—I never got it—it's not true.

(*Both* BEAUREVERS *and* SEVIGNE *take it for granted that she is only defending her lover, as before.*)

BEAUREVERS. (*To* JOSEFA.) Let us not confuse each other—over trifles, my dear—
JOSEFA. (*Rises.*) But I didn't get the note—I knew nothing about meeting at eleven—
SEVIGNE. (*Wrathfully.*) Out! (*Pointing.*) Morestan, call the guard and ask him to—
JOSEFA. No, no. I won't interrupt again. I swear it. (*Sits.*)

(*And as* SEVIGNE *subsides, nodding to* MORESTAN.)

BEAUREVERS. You see, the chauffeur was already out of the way—my wife decided to stay with her friends for dinner— (*With a shrug and a smile.*) Why grow old waiting?
SEVIGNE. Why, indeed? (*And then.*) Your conversations with the cook, and at the club, those indicate quite a degree of feeling, don't they?
JOSEFA. I tell you he must have been drinking.
BEAUREVERS. All right, Josefa. That's enough. It's not important.
JOSEFA. It is. He's *accusing* you! *Tell him!*
SEVIGNE. Actually, Monsieur Beaurevers is accusing himself— (*Holding the document.*) "To keep her I would

be capable of anything—even divorce—even a crime." *Is that how you feel?*

JOSEFA. (*To* SEVIGNE.) No, it isn't. I'm like that! You said so yourself! But him—*never!*

SEVIGNE. (*To* BEAUREVERS, *formally.*) I think it's time you spoke for yourself. How *do* you feel?

BEAUREVERS. (*Quietly.*) This is how: I have a brutal, raging need of her. She *is* in my blood, like a fever that sets me trembling. (SEVIGNE *is surprised, a little embarrassed by the outburst;* JOSEFA *is puzzled, too worried, momentarily, to really understand what he is saying. Rises, free movement.*) It's a craving. I'm addicted to her. When I'm deprived of the relief that only she can give me, a dull aching pain settles in the back of my skull, and throbs there, hammering at me. (JOSEFA *looks confused, frightened.*) But I don't *love* her! (*This hits her, hard.*) I feel nothing for her except my need of her. Is that love? Is an addict in love with his heroin or cocaine?

JOSEFA. (*Hurt, whimpering.*) No—don't say it—please!

BEAUREVERS. I must. (*He turns his back on* JOSEFA, *facing* SEVIGNE.) I don't care what you think or what you suspect. I'm saying this to break the relationship, to be free. Do you think I would kill Ostos . . . divorce my wife . . . and then what? Live with her—torn between her embarrassed silence and insane, explosive jealousy? To be perpetually at the mercy of her mood? No! No, thank you! In time, I think, I could have killed. But only one of us. Josefa or myself. That at least would buy me back my freedom, but killing Ostos to have her for myself—that meant slavery.

JOSEFA. (*After a silence.*) I want very much to faint—very much— (*She sways a bit, but that's all.*)

SEVIGNE. (*To* BEAUREVERS.) Well, your relationship is clarified, I guess—

JOSEFA. (*Shivering.*) It's cold here—

BEAUREVERS. I had to do it. (*Without looking at her.*) I'm sorry, Josefa.

JOSEFA. Miguel, at least, only hit me with his fist.
BEAUREVERS. (*To* SEVIGNE.) Can I go now?
SEVIGNE. In a moment. (*His TELEPHONE rings.*) Just let me— Damn! (*Snatches it, irritably.*) Sevigne speaking— (*And in an entirely different tone.*) Yes, sir. Yes, thank you, sir, I'll be delighted to have your opinion. (*Helplessly.*) Go right ahead, sir. (*Listens impatiently, not daring to interrupt, fidgeting and twisting in his chair.*)
JOSEFA. (*To* BEAUREVERS.) I was ashamed of my ignorance—I used to wish that you'd speak simply, so I could understand— (*With a deep sigh.*) Well, *finally!* (*At his unbending back; rises.*) Turn around—you used to swallow me with your eyes. At least look at me now! (SEVIGNE, *listening, gestures frantically for silence.*) Liar! (*And then, wounded.*) Does an addict love his drug? Now, that's a pretty speech I'll always remember!
SEVIGNE. (*Into the telephone.*) No, sir, I didn't say *anything.* I have some people here and— (*Then resigned again.*) Yes, sir, I'm listening. (*And he does.*)
JOSEFA. (*Paces* L. *and* R.) I wanted you to need me— the way I needed you—not on prescription, like a painkiller. Forgive me for the headaches I gave you. And if I meant so much to you, forgive me for that, too— (*Softly, deeply hurt.*) And for having pleased you so much! (*And then, angrily.*) My God, what lies! Liar! Liar!

(BEAUREVERS *sits.* SEVIGNE *gestures frantically for silence.*)

SEVIGNE. (*Into the telephone.*) No, sir, I didn't say anything. I'm listening.
JOSEFA. (*Steaming.*) You used to whisper that I gave you wings—you said my body was a launching-pad for a rocket of dreams. What kind of a drug is *that?* You've gotten rid of that dull aching pain at the back of the skull, haven't you? I've got it now. You gave it to me.
SEVIGNE. (*Covering the mouthpiece.*) Stop it—I can't

hear— (*Into the telephone.*) Yes, sir, that's my opinion, too—

JOSEFA. (*Going right on.*) The village idiot, that's me. I believed everything. (*Mimicking.*) "My wife doesn't understand me." *Nobody* believes *that* any more. And I believed it. (*Mimicking.*) "I need you, Josefa. My wife and I live like brother and sister. And I have nobody." And I believed even *that*. I *knew* it was a lie, and I believed it.

SEVIGNE. (*Covering the mouthpiece.*) A little less noise if you please! I am talking to the Chief Prosecutor. (*And into the telephone.*) Yes, sir, I'm listening. (*He is torn in fact as* JOSEFA *continues her tirade between listening to the Chief and to what she is saying.*)

JOSEFA. (*Bitterly.*) Those poker games that went on all night at your Club! How many times I lay weeping at your lies and heard you creeping into the house, tiptoeing upstairs to *her*. (BEAUREVERS *has stiffened like a ramrod at this. He wheels slowly, like a piece of heavy artillery.*) Sneaking up the stairs— (*With utter contempt.*) to your wife.

BEAUREVERS. (*Oddly strained.*) What are you saying?

JOSEFA. Liar! And what a cheap, stupid lie! (BEAUREVERS *shakes his head, puzzled. She continues hotly.*) Do you deny it? Just last week—Tuesday—another all-night game—but before midnight you were creeping up the stairs—to her.

BEAUREVERS. (*With some difficulty.*) Tuesday—I played until 7 o'clock in the morning. I lost 20,000 francs. *New* francs.

JOSEFA. (*With contempt.*) Stop it! I heard your key in the lock—then your footsteps, quietly, going upstairs— (*The look on* BEAUREVERS' *face puzzles her.*)

BEAUREVERS. (*Hoarse.*) Who was it? Who was the man?

JOSEFA. (*But uncertainly now.*) It was you—who else could open the front door with a key—every time you had an all-night poker-game? (*And then, backing* L., *horrified by what she has revealed.*) Oh!

BEAUREVERS. (*Rises.*) Dominique!

SEVIGNE. (*Into the telephone, frantically.*) Chief, if I could call you back—I think there is an important development— (*And then frustrated, listening.*) Yes, sir.

BEAUREVERS. Dominique! (*He slowly massages the back of his skull.*) My wife!—my head! (*Weakly, to* JOSEFA.) Every time I played poker? (*Plaintively.*) You're sure? (*And then, a groan.*) Dominique! (*Again massaging his skull, sits.*)

SEVIGNE. (*Into the telephone.*) Yes, sir, of course, I know what the Beaurevers family stands for— (*Listens for a beat.*) Madame Beaurevers, too—yes, sir— (*Listens for another beat, glancing up at* BEAUREVERS.) His position? Yes, sir— (BEAUREVERS *is massaging his skull again, slowly, painfully.*) I particularly know what *he* stands for— (*Thoughtfully, as he hangs up.*) So does he.

(*It has taken* JOSEFA *a few moments to realize that this is her revenge, and she breaks suddenly into wild laughter.* BEAUREVERS *is still massaging his skull as:*)

THE CURTAIN FALLS

ACT THREE

THE TIME: *The same day, between five and six p.m.*
AT RISE: SEVIGNE *is at his desk, as is* MORESTAN. LA-
BLACHE, *in a state of considerable agitation, is pacing. Pacing is not easy in these cramped quarters, but he does the best he can. He is plainly not overfond of* SEVIGNE *at this moment.* MORESTAN *is studying his notes,* SEVIGNE *is studying* LABLACHE, LA-
BLACHE *is pacing.*

LABLACHE. (*Pacing* D. L.; *then to* R. *Finally.*) Really! I must say, Sevigne, that you surprise me. (*With some bitterness.*) Forty-eight hours ago I gave you an assignment about as innocent of repercussions as a grocer charged with blocking the sidewalk. Two days—two little days—and suddenly we have something like the Dreyfus case on our hands. You are pursuing a very dangerous course.

SEVIGNE. Do I have any choice?

LABLACHE. (*Shakes his head, rather pityingly.*) All right—let's examine the revised situation. It would appear that you have uncovered some indiscretion on the part of Madame Beaurevers—

SEVIGNE. (*Bluntly.*) She had a lover.

LABLACHE. Horrible! Nobody in Paris would believe such a thing!

SEVIGNE. I didn't find the news overwhelming, but the husband involved—well, you should have seen Beaurevers when it hit him!

LABLACHE. And for that very reason, I urge you not to believe too much. Husbands—even wives, in such circumstances—are notoriously vindictive.

SEVIGNE. I'm aware of that.

LABLACHE. Furthermore, to conclude that such a situation inevitably leads to murder is sheer insanity. My

God, if that were true, you'd hear nothing but gunfire all day long and the streets of Paris would be choked with funeral processions.

SEVIGNE. I draw no conclusions. I prefer that you judge the testimony for yourself.

LABLACHE. (*Sits U. R. desk; reluctantly.*) All right.

SEVIGNE. (*To* MORESTAN.) Ready?

MORESTAN. Yes, sir. (*Clears his throat importantly. At* SEVIGNE'S *gesture, he starts to read from his notes. He reads slowly, clearly and distinctly, in a monotone, with no expression whatever.*)

Question: "Are you now prepared to make a new statement?"

Answer: "Yes. I want to settle with that bitch."

LABLACHE. What?

MORESTAN. Excuse me, I'm only reading.

LABLACHE. He used that word?

SEVIGNE. His speech became surprisingly colloquial. (*To* MORESTAN.) Go on.

MORESTAN. (*Reading.*) "It was not I who first reached the scene of the crime—it was my wife."

LABLACHE. What? (*And as* SEVIGNE *nods, he goes on grimly.*) Does he explain his original statement?

SEVIGNE. Go on, Morestan.

MORESTAN. (*In the same old monotone.*)

Question: "Why did you previously state that you were the first to arrive?"

Answer: "It was my wife's idea."

LABLACHE. (*Skeptically.*) Ha! (MORESTAN *gives him a reproving look.*)

MORESTAN. (*Reading.*)

Question: "Why did you agree to this if it was not true?"

Answer: "I was completely bewildered and I had complete confidence in Dominique. Besides, I thought that if I said I was the first, I could help Josefa by suppressing the statement Dominique told me Ostos made when he was dying, in which he accused Josefa of the shooting."

LABLACHE. (*Pained, grudgingly.*) Is that true?

SEVIGNE. Inspector Colas confirms that Beaurevers

withheld that information until it was dropped by Madame. (*And as* LABLACHE *groans, he gestures to* MORESTAN *to continue.*)

MORESTAN. (*Reading.*)
Question: "What did you see when you entered the room?"
Answer: "My wife bending over Josefa, who was unconscious on the floor. I believed what she told me then—that Josefa had killed her lover, but I think now that she was just putting the revolver in Josefa's hand."

LABLACHE. (*Hoping against hope.*) As I warned you, the words of a vindictive husband.

(*He relapses into silence, shaking his head. At a sign from* SEVIGNE, MORESTAN *picks up the narration.*)

MORESTAN. Question: "Ostos was much taller than you. How is it possible that your wife could have mistaken him for you?"

LABLACHE. (*Warmly.*) Ah, an excellent point.

MORESTAN. (*Reading.*)
Answer: "It was due to modesty."
Question: "Whose modesty?"
Answer: "Ostos' modesty. The room was in total darkness. My wife fired at a shadow she thought was mine. Poor Ostos, if he were at all like me, he would be alive today, because in such circumstances, *I* like to see what I'm doing."

(*Apologetically to* LABLACHE.) Excuse me— (*Indicating his notes.*) —I'm only reading.

LABLACHE. Go on!

MORESTAN. (*Reading.*) "But for Ostos' modesty, my wife would now be a rich, beautiful, young widow. A decent interval of mourning—Dominique looks marvellous in black, by the way—and she would be free to marry her lover."
Question: "Who is the man?"
Answer: "Monsieur Jean-Claude de Benoit, 139 rue de

Varenne, Paris, 7th Arrondissement. Telephone: Invalides 28-93."

Question: "How is it that you're so certain?"

Answer: "He is my best friend."

SEVIGNE. Charming lot, your Beaurevers!

LABLACHE. (*Rises, crosses* D. R. *to window.*) They are not my Beaurevers. And so far, what they've done is not illegal—it's not even unpopular. (*Curtly, to* MORESTAN.) Go on. (*Sits at window,* R.)

MORESTAN. (*Reading.*)

Question: "There is no doubt in your mind that Monsieur de Benoit is the man?"

Answer: "None whatever. He and my wife were inseparable due to their mutual passion for horses—or so I thought. He spent all the holidays with us at Hauterive—hunting, riding, racing. Now I remember how many times, when they came back from the trails, *they* were exhausted, and the horses were fresh."

Question: "Do you now formally accuse your wife of murdering Ostos?"

Answer: "I do."

SEVIGNE. Well, that's certainly illegal, and probably unpopular.

LABLACHE. She makes the same accusation against him, doesn't she?

SEVIGNE. He adds a few details, some of them quite convincing. The gloves, Morestan.

MORESTAN. Coming up. (*He riffles the pages of his book to find the appropriate page, then locating it, clears his throat.*)

Question: "Do you actually believe that your wife planned a cold-blooded, premeditated murder?"

Answer: "Ha!"

(*Apologetically, to* LABLACHE.) H-A, and an exclamation— (*And then from his notes.*)

Question: "Can you be more precise?"

Answer: "She got the note I intended for Josefa, and she expected to find me in the room. Furthermore, I call to your attention that she was still wearing her gloves, so that her fingerprints would not appear on the gun or anywhere in the room."

LABLACHE. (*Pained*.) In the police interrogation did he not mention that she was wearing her gloves?

SEVIGNE. No. (*Gestures to* MORESTAN *to continue*.)

MORESTAN.
Question: "Why did you withhold this information from the police?"
Answer: "Because it didn't seem important."
Question: "Why does it seem important now?"
Answer: "When a wife has a lover, *all* her actions seem more important."

LABLACHE. (*Involuntarily*.) God knows, that's true! (*Rises; crosses Up; and then*.) But it has no legal bearing whatsoever. I'm sure she had reasonable explanations for everything. (*Pleadingly*.) Didn't she? (*Turns Down; sits* U. L.)

SEVIGNE. She was fantastically good. Poised, calm, serene—sat there like Whistler's Mother, dressed by Balanciaga. And then suddenly, a tiny crack in that glossy surface— (*With a gesture to* MORESTAN, *who reads as before*.)

MORESTAN. Question: "Did you wear gloves that night, Madame?"

SEVIGNE. This was followed by a terrible silence.

MORESTAN. I made a note. Silence. Then, finally, answer: "It's possible. I had just come in from outdoors. I heard the shot and it's possible that I didn't pause to take off my gloves."

SEVIGNE. Now she suddenly realized that her husband had talked. (*Nods to* MORESTAN.)

MORESTAN.
Question: "You seem pale, Madame—would you like a glass of water?" Drinks.
Answer: "No. If I am pale, it is because of the strain on me, but I can no longer conceal the truth. I love my husband, whatever his shortcomings, but I have endured too much. . . ."

SEVIGNE. Here her voice broke, and, very reluctantly,

she told *her* story. Read us that tender chapter in the home-life of the Beaurevers family, Morestan.

MORESTAN.
Question: "On entering the room, what did you see?"
Answer: "Ostos was lying dead on the floor and my husband was on his knees beside Josefa. At my entrance, he gave a wild cry of alarm, like some trapped animal. I was terrified. And in my panic, with his frenzied pleadings in my ears, I became his accomplice. I was *not* wearing my gloves, but he used them to wipe the finger-prints from the weapon, then *he* put it in Josefa's hand."

LABLACHE. (*Rises; crosses* C.) God, you read badly!

MORESTAN. (*Defensively.*) I'm a clerk; I read like a clerk.

SEVIGNE. Perhaps you'd like to hear what went on when they were finally face to face?

LABLACHE. No, no—spare me. (*He gets up, paces around nervously again, then timidly.*) They—they actually repeated their accusations then?

SEVIGNE. Savagely. They shouted unprintable things at one another. Monstrous accusations. And then— (*With a shrug, producing two documents with seals affixed.*) they signed them.

LABLACHE. (*Utter unenthusiasm.*) Good work! Splendid! (*And then, wanly.*) Identical confessions—they accuse each other—not very conclusive, is it?

SEVIGNE. Not so far.

LABLACHE. (*He has a thoughtful moment. Crosses* L. *to Morestan's desk.*) Er—Morestan, would you mind stepping over to the Second Tribunal and waiting for the verdict in the Trévillon case? Let me know what happens.

MORESTAN. Yes, sir. (*He goes.*)

(LABLACHE *starts pacing again,* SEVIGNE *watching him.*)

LABLACHE. (*Crosses* D. L.) We want to give this some thought, don't we? (*And as* SEVIGNE *nods.*) Ostos is dead —the girl is unconscious— (*Crosses* C.; *ticking them off on two fingers.*) The husband and wife accuse each other and generally speaking, that cancels their testimony. Result—*no* witnesses.

SEVIGNE. That's true.

LABLACHE. (*Crosses* R.; *pressing his advantage.*) Husband and wife—that's tricky business. I'm a husband myself, and I've got a wife—I know.

SEVIGNE. Has your wife ever tried to murder you?

LABLACHE. (*Crosses to Sevigne's desk.*) Now, wait. That is not yet an established fact. And besides, he hasn't quite been the Husband of the Year himself, has he?

SEVIGNE. No. But what she planned was a cold-blooded assassination—for profit.

LABLACHE. Stop harping on that. Can you prove it?

SEVIGNE. (*Reluctantly.*) No—not yet.

LABLACHE. Well, then— (*And then, indicating the Beaurevers' statements.*) How much of all this does Josefa Lantenay know?

SEVIGNE. So far, nothing.

LABLACHE. (*Gratified.*) Ah! (*Wistfully.*) But she has a lawyer now, hasn't she?

SEVIGNE. I assigned one, but she wouldn't see him or have anything to do with him.

LABLACHE. (*Gratified; casually.*) How do you plan to proceed?

SEVIGNE. (*Just as casually.*) To begin with, we might as well let the girl go.

LABLACHE. (*Nodding.*) H-m-m-m-m—

SEVIGNE. That *is* the first step, isn't it?

LABLACHE. If you release the girl, the case explodes at once. (*At* SEVIGNE'S *shrug.*) The newspapers are whispering already. With the girl cleared, they'd roar.

SEVIGNE. I suppose so—yes.

LABLACHE. Scandal is mud. Give it time to dry and it turns to dust. Then deal with it.

SEVIGNE. To protect the Beaurevers?

LABLACHE. (*Crosses* C.) Yes, damn it! Oh, I know it isn't equal justice under law, but the Beaurevers just aren't equal. (*With a shrug.*) Condemn me if you like— I'm afraid of them.

SEVIGNE. (*Troubled.*) So am I.

LABLACHE. (*Ingenuously.*) And what's the harm, finally? If this case remains an affair of a chauffeur and a maid, I give you my word that in two months' time it won't matter to anyone. (*Crosses* R.)

SEVIGNE. Except, of course, to the maid.

LABLACHE. In the long run, even she'll be better off without a scandal trailing along behind her.

SEVIGNE. (*Thoughtfully.*) Lablache, have you ever been in a women's prison?

LABLACHE. (*Surprised.*) Eh? Why?

SEVIGNE. Oh, I just wondered what you thought of conditions in them?

LABLACHE. (*Nettled.*) No, I have not been in a women's prison. (*Crosses* C.; *pointedly.*) Also I am not a parlormaid who sleeps with the Spanish chauffeur *and* her boss. Wake up, Sevigne—the girl isn't so much of an ingenue that you must act like a juvenile.

SEVIGNE. (*Thoughtfully.*) Two months, you say?

LABLACHE. Not even that. Six weeks.

SEVIGNE. Six weeks? (*And then.*) No, damn it, I can't!

LABLACHE. A month.

SEVIGNE. No! Not one day! Why should the girl pay for the Beaurevers? Because they're so much richer than she is?

LABLACHE. (*Nods resignedly, rises.*) You'll be finished today?

SEVIGNE. Are you asking me?—or telling me? (LABLACHE *shrugs.*) I hope to be finished today—yes.

LABLACHE. (*He nods, starts out* U. C. *Stops before reaching the door. Resigned.*) Well, then, that's that. (*And then, shrewdly.*) In coming to a decision, have you thought of your wife? (*At* SEVIGNE's *glance.*) I mean, she is involved in your future, isn't she?

SEVIGNE. Yes, very much so. (*And then, stoutly.*) Whatever I do, I know I can count on Antoinette.

LABLACHE. Ah, well, you're a lucky man— (*He starts out, pausing before he goes.*) Good luck then, Sevigne — *with everything.*

ACT III   A SHOT IN THE DARK   75

(LABLACHE *leaves.* SEVIGNE, *left alone, doesn't seem quite so sure of himself. A couple of times he reaches for the 'phone and then pulls back as though unwilling to make the test, but finally he takes it, dials a number.*)

SEVIGNE. Lablache!—Hello—Antoinette?—How are you, darling?—No, I'm fine— I had a few minutes between chores—the case?—Well, I think it's going very well, but there seems to be a difference of opinion— (*He braces himself for a moment.*) I may be taken off it before the day is over. (*He listens, smiling for the first time.*) The Chief Prosecutor is a *what?* (*Delighted.*) Antoinette, where did you ever learn such a word? (*Then, crestfallen.*) Oh, that's what your mother used to call *me?* (*Then, soberly.*) Antoinette, what if your mother were right—I mean, if things were rough for a while: no new apartment, or car—? (*He smiles, then, listening, and his smile becomes wider and wider, and he says softly.*) Thank you, darling. (*He puts down the 'phone. His dejection is gone. He turns back to his desk and the work as* MORESTAN *enters.*)

MORESTAN. (*Crosses* R. *above.*) Lablache is gone? You seem pretty cheerful. (*Shrugs off his apathy.*)

SEVIGNE. We'd better get back to work. Lablache implied that if I wanted to finish on this case, I'd better work fast.

MORESTAN. (*Moves chair back* U. R.; *casually.*) Yes, that's the rumor in the building. (*As* SEVIGNE *glances up at him.*) The girl is waiting. Want her?

SEVIGNE. How is she behaving?

MORESTAN. Hard to tell. She's sound asleep on a bench.

SEVIGNE. It seems to be a lot less strain on her than on me. Yes, get her in. (MORESTAN *goes out, returning in a moment with* JOSEFA. *She is rubbing her eyes, as if from a sleep, and she looks around the office eagerly, apparently a bit let down at finding herself alone with the two men.* MORESTAN *sits* L.) Expecting someone?

JOSEFA. (*At* C.) No. (*She seems very subdued.*)

SEVIGNE. Sit down.

JOSEFA. (*She takes the indicated chair, folding her coat over the back. Once or twice she seems about to speak, doesn't quite make it. Then, finally.*) Monsieur has gone?

SEVIGNE. Monsieur?

JOSEFA. Monsieur Beaurevers? (*And then a groan.*) Oh-h-h-h-h! (*Holding her head.*) *My* big mouth: I'm even worse than the cook! (*Plaintively.*) And he *was* playing poker all night long. (*Exasperated.*) Does telling the truth ever help anybody?

SEVIGNE. In my official capacity I don't think I ought to answer that.

JOSEFA. He—he was terribly upset, wasn't he?

SEVIGNE. Reasonably. (*He watches her. She is nervous, fidgeting, bracing herself for something.*) What's wrong with you?

JOSEFA. Nothing—now. It's over. I want to confess.

SEVIGNE. (*Startled.*) What!

(*And there is an involuntary exclamation from* MORESTAN.)

JOSEFA. I'm just not bright enough to keep track of all my lies. The strain is too much. I want to confess.

SEVIGNE. Anything special?

JOSEFA. I killed Miguel. (MORESTAN *drops his pen, with an exclamation. She turns to him.*) Write! Take it down! (*Rises. As* MORESTAN *stares at her.*) You've been writing down even my sneezes for two days, and suddenly you're helpless. *I'm confessing!*

SEVIGNE. Here—look at me! (*She turns* R., *warily defiant.*) Why are you being such an idiot?

JOSEFA. A conscience that jabs me like a red-hot spear —you call that idiotic?

SEVIGNE. If you're still protecting Monsieur Beaurevers, let me tell you—

JOSEFA. Protecting *him?* After what you heard him say to me in this room?

SEVIGNE. All right. Go on. Take it, Morestan.

JOSEFA. Thank you. (*Sits. She swallows, braces herself.*) I killed Miguel—I shot him—with the pistol kept in the Rolls-Royce—

SEVIGNE. Which Rolls-Royce?

JOSEFA. The limousine.

SEVIGNE. Go on.

JOSEFA. I shot him—of course, I didn't mean to kill him—only to wound him—but there you are— (*She is running out of steam—plaintively.*) Don't you want to ask me any questions?

SEVIGNE. And interrupt you in the middle of your confession?

JOSEFA. (*Wistfully.*) I don't mind.

SEVIGNE. Well, *why* did you kill him?

JOSEFA. Ah! (*She is ready for this one.*) His brutality. He beat me. You know that from witnesses, don't you? Well, that night again, because he was suspicious—

SEVIGNE. You had no bruises—

JOSEFA. He held me by the hair and beat my head against the floor. That's how I got this bump. I thought he meant to kill me. So I fired. (*Glances to see if* MORESTAN *has it all, then sighs.*) I feel better now.

SEVIGNE. Where was the revolver?

JOSEFA. When I shot him—in my hand, of course.

SEVIGNE. No—I mean, where did you have it in your room? (*As she looks at him unhappily.*) In a drawer?—in your purse?—in the bed?—*under* the bed?

JOSEFA. (*Eagerly.*) Under the bed. I reached for it. I hardly knew what I was doing, he was giving me such a thumping—

SEVIGNE. (*Mildly.*) The shot was fired at a distance of at least ten feet.

JOSEFA. I—I—I broke away from him— (*Inspiration.*) The gun was under the other side of the bed.

SEVIGNE. How did it get there?

JOSEFA. We struggled for it—I knocked it out of his hand—it fell to the floor and—I kicked it. (MORESTAN *is listening open-mouthed. She adds plaintively.*) He's not writing anything!

SEVIGNE. (*With a sigh.*) All right, Morestan. Take it down, just as she told it. There is no longer any case against Madame Beaurevers.

JOSEFA. (*Humbly.*) I'm sorry I didn't confess right away— (*She looks from one to the other.*) Madame Beaurevers! I thought it was *him*.

SEVIGNE. (*Severely.*) That's none of your business. Go on with your confession. (*And as* JOSEFA *hesitates in painful uncertainty.*) Where's that red-hot spear of conscience that was jabbing you a minute ago?

JOSEFA. (*Uncertainly.*) It sort of comes and goes— (*Looks pleadingly at* SEVIGNE.) What's this about Madame?

SEVIGNE. (*Tinged with pity.*) Idiot!

JOSEFA. (*Humbly.*) I know. (*She waits for him to go on.*)

SEVIGNE. It seems that it was Madame Beaurevers who was first in the room after the shooting. *She* found you.

JOSEFA. (*Embarrassed.*) Madame? (*She tugs her skirt down.*) But *he* heard Miguel accuse me—his last words— (*And as* SEVIGNE *shakes his head, delighted.*) Oh! (*Impulsively* JOSEFA *rises, takes his hand and kisses it. Surprised,* SEVIGNE *backs away from her quickly.*) Then he *didn't* die thinking I shot him! Oh, thank you! Thank you for that! (*Then suddenly wounded.*) Monsieur Beaurevers used *that* against me—?

SEVIGNE. He thought it was true. It was his wife who said she heard Ostos accuse you.

JOSEFA. (*Delighted again, looking up.*) Miguel, do you hear? Are you listening, my poor Miguel? (*To* SEVIGNE *wistfully.*) Do you think he *is* listening somewhere—do you think he knows now that I'm innocent?

SEVIGNE. (*Kindly.*) Perhaps. I hope so.

JOSEFA. (*Wistfully.*) Innocent or not, if he could get his hands on me right now, I'd get a good clip on the ear. (*Looking up.*) Forgive me, Miguel. I should have known it was you who really loved me.

SEVIGNE. When you've finished with the spirit world, I'd like to get back to business.

JOSEFA. Did she kill Miguel? (*Awed, rocking in surprise and a touch of admiration.*) That crazy Spaniard? He and Madame—*also?* (*Sits.*)

SEVIGNE. No.

JOSEFA. (*Skeptically.*) They weren't—not *anything?*

SEVIGNE. She expected to find her husband in your room.

JOSEFA. (*Shocked.*) Oh! (*Wincing.*) Poor Miguel! He died by mistake—like a wrong number! (*Rises, crosses* C. *Impulsively, passionately.*) Punish her! Put her in prison! She can have my room!

SEVIGNE. Well—

JOSEFA. You must. (*Crosses* R. *Earnestly.*) Miguel must be avenged. To a Spaniard these things are terribly important. You must punish her! I'm not asking for myself —for Miguel. I'll help you.

SEVIGNE. Thank you. That's just what I need. You deny everything, you confess everything. You're really a big help! (*Turns away.*)

JOSEFA. I'm sorry. But please let me help—

SEVIGNE. Shut up. I'm thinking. Do you know her wardrobe?

JOSEFA. Oh, yes.

SEVIGNE. Everything?

JOSEFA. Every stitch. Even her underwear! (*Rubs her hands.*) Do you want me to search her?

SEVIGNE. Stop babbling! (*Pointing to a corner far* D. L.) Sit over there.

JOSEFA. Yes, sir. (*Going obediently to her corner far* D. L.; *sits.*)

SEVIGNE. Sit still, and listen.

(*When she is settled in her corner, he nods to* MORESTAN, *pointing to exit, who rises and goes to the door, admitting* MADAME BEAUREVERS. *She makes her accustomed sweeping entrance.*)

MADAME BEAUREVERS. Well, at last!

SEVIGNE. (*Who has risen politely.*) I'm sorry to have kept you waiting. Please sit down.

MADAME BEAUREVERS. (*At c.; graciously, but still grand.*) Thank you. (*And in turning.*) Ah, Josefa! (*Looking her up and down.*) I must say, prison seems to agree with you.

(MORESTAN *sits again.*)

JOSEFA. Thank you, Madame. (*And pointedly.*) It's possible to get used to anything.

SEVIGNE. And now, Madame, there are a few questions I would like to clear up.

MADAME BEAUREVERS. Very well. (*Sits in witness chair.*)

(SEVIGNE *takes the file and* JOSEFA *beams approval. He leaves a pregnant, hushed pause, designed to crack the witness's nerve, but* MADAME BEAUREVERS *calmly takes a gold compact from her purse and powders her nose with a steady hand.* SEVIGNE *looks dismayed and* JOSEFA *nods fiercely, urging him to the "attack."* MADAME BEAUREVERS *deliberately uses a gold lipstick, after which she puts her apparatus away.*)

SEVIGNE. Who is Monsieur Jean-Claude de Benoit?

MADAME BEAUREVERS. (*Calmly.*) A childhood friend.

SEVIGNE. (*Mildly.*) Children grow up—they learn new games— (JOSEFA *is gesturing as with a sword: "Attack, attack!"* SEVIGNE *has whisked a paper deftly from the file.*) Three months ago, when you returned from the country, you yourself ordered a new key to the front door of your house. (*And as the* WITNESS' *composure is momentarily bruised.*) Why?

MADAME BEAUREVERS. I—I had lost mine—I wanted to replace it.

SEVIGNE. (*From the paper.*) But the locksmith swears—

(*Rattling the paper.*) that you had your key; that in fact you gave it to him so that he could copy it. *Why?*

MADAME BEAUREVERS. I must have wanted—needed— a duplicate.

SEVIGNE. Where is it now?

MADAME BEAUREVERS. I don't know. I may have misplaced it. (*Gathering anger.*) Really! It seems to be a great fuss about nothing at all!

SEVIGNE. Yes, of course. Childhood friends! Nothing more natural than that Monsieur de Benoit should have a key of his own and come and go as he pleased.

MADAME BEAUREVERS. (*Indifferently.*) Think what you like. It is of no importance.

SEVIGNE. I am content that you should be the judge of that, Madame. However, we are investigating a murder, and this bears directly on your own motive.

JOSEFA. (*Rises; explosively.*) Ole! Ole! (SEVIGNE *glares at her and* MADAME BEAUREVERS *turns slowly; she subsides.*) I—I was thinking of something else—excuse me.

MADAME BEAUREVERS. Thinking of something else! Does she *ever* think of anything else? Frankly, then: my husband and this unwashed rabbit were carrying on— under my own roof, humiliating me before my own servants. Very well. I found a means of consolation. That is the extent of my crime. You may investigate it, if you like, until Doomsday.

SEVIGNE. I think we can drop the matter. (JOSEFA *seems pained and crosses* U. L.) Except for one minor point. (JOSEFA *turns* R.; *brightens.*) Do you have money of your own, Madame?

MADAME BEAUREVERS. (*Stiffly.*) Really! I am not considering opening an account here, you know— (JOSEFA *sits* U. L. *Under* SEVIGNE's *steady, waiting stare.*) We are a very old and, if I may say so, distinguished family. Not merchants or bankers.

SEVIGNE. In other words, you are dependent on Monsieur Beaurevers— (*She shrugs it off.*) You knew from the servants' gossip, did you not, that your husband visited Josefa from time to time?

(JOSEFA *looks demure, tugging down her skirt.*)

MADAME BEAUREVERS. (*Contemptuously.*) Yes, of course.
SEVIGNE. Did you know when?
MADAME BEAUREVERS. No.
SEVIGNE. In the early afternoon on the day of the shooting, your husband sent Josefa a note fixing a rendezous for ten o'clock that night. She never got the note. Do you know anything about that, Madame?
MADAME BEAUREVERS. Nothing whatever.
SEVIGNE. You dined with friends that night?
MADAME BEAUREVERS. Yes. Monsieur and Madame Belvoir.
SEVIGNE. Was that a long-standing invitation?
MADAME BEAUREVERS. No—actually it was arranged that same day.
SEVIGNE. Was it at their suggestion—or yours?
MADAME BEAUREVERS. I—I don't remember. We are very old friends—what possible difference can it make?
SEVIGNE. (*Gently.*) If you *had* intercepted your husband's note, and knew he was to be in Josefa's room at ten o'clock, you might have wanted him to have the illusion that he had—so to speak—a clear field. (*She looks at him steadily, coldly.*) It is only a suggestion. (*And then, finding a new place in his file.*) When was the last time you used the Rolls-Royce limousine?
MADAME BEAUREVERS. The limousine?—let me see—
JOSEFA. (*Respectfully.*) The night before, Madame, for the gala—
MADAME BEAUREVERS. Ah, yes. My husband and I went to a diplomatic gala at the Opera.
JOSEFA. (*Rises.*) Madame wore a ballgown. Grey satin, with a train— (*Swishing it about in pantomime.*) she looked lovely in it. (SEVIGNE *looks puzzled; she goes on*

artlessly.) The next morning, even before I did the room, it had already been sent to the cleaners.

MADAME BEAUREVERS. A long skirt—someone probably stepped on it in the crush at the intermission.

JOSEFA. All afternoon—before the gala—Miguel was working on a leak in the crankcase of the limousine. The floor of the garage was covered with grease. And he didn't finish in time to clean it up.

SEVIGNE. Who does your cleaning, Madame?

MADAME BEAUREVERS. (*Reluctantly.*) I—I have the name written down at home—

JOSEFA. (*Cheerfully.*) Lacoste and Bergerie, Cleaners and Dyers, 56 avenue Victor Hugo. "Clothes dyed Black for Mourning in 24 Hours," Madame.

(JOSEFA *sits. Under* SEVIGNE's *steady stare,* MADAME BEAUREVERS *shifts a bit uneasily.*)

SEVIGNE. Was there grease on the skirt of your ball-gown, Madame?

MADAME BEAUREVERS. I—I did go to the garage that night—after we returned from the gala—I realized that I had left my gloves in the car—forgot them—

SEVIGNE. Did you find them?

MADAME BEAUREVERS. Yes.

SEVIGNE. Where?

MADAME BEAUREVERS. In the glove-compartment, where I had put them. That's what a glove-compartment is for, isn't it?

SEVIGNE. (*Mildly.*) In this particular glove-compartment there also happened to be a fully-loaded revolver.

MADAME BEAUREVERS. No. (*And at* SEVIGNE's *surprise.*) It was no longer there.

SEVIGNE. I see. Did you mention the disappearance of this weapon?

MADAME BEAUREVERS. As a matter of fact, I did. I asked Miguel in the morning and he told me that my husband had taken it. There was no longer any need to keep it in the car, he said, and he would return it to the bank.

SEVIGNE. It would help if this could be verified, but Ostos, unfortunately, is dead.

MADAME BEAUREVERS. (*Coolly.*) We all have to go when our time comes.

SEVIGNE. At any rate, you found your gloves, so the trip to the garage was not a total loss.

JOSEFA. And they were such beautiful, long gloves, buttoning up to the elbow—not the kind that are easy to put on and take off.

MADAME BEAUREVERS. (*Snapping.*) Well, I did. They were tight and uncomfortable—and I wanted to smoke.

SEVIGNE. Sitting with your husband, in the back seat of the limousine?—and you put your gloves in the compartment—*up front?*

(*There is unmistakably the feeling that Sevigne has sprung the trap.* MORESTAN, JOSEFA, SEVIGNE *himself are all poised for the "kill."*)

MADAME BEAUREVERS. (*Calmly.*) We gave some friends a lift home in the car. There were six of us in all. My husband and I both sat in front. Ask him. He will confirm it.

(SEVIGNE *is pained, and except for* MADAME BEAUREVERS *there is general deflation.*)

SEVIGNE. Touché!

MADAME BEAUREVERS. (*Relentlessly.*) I am telling the truth. When I entered the room Ostos was dead, and my husband was kneeling beside your charming assistant— (*Indicating* JOSEFA.) naked as a plucked chicken, in a faint.

JOSEFA. The traffic in my room that night! (*Tugging at her skirt.*) Like the Place de la Concorde!

SEVIGNE. Are you quite sure, Madame, that you mentioned the disappearance of the gun to Ostos?

MADAME BEAUREVERS. Oh, yes, I remember it clearly.

SEVIGNE. Since you did not then know *who* had taken the weapon, why did you not speak of it to your husband?

MADAME BEAUREVERS. I meant to, in fact, but when I woke up the next morning he had already gone to the bank.

(JOSEFA *rises, is gesturing frantically to the clock.*)

SEVIGNE. What time did you wake up, Madame?

MADAME BEAUREVERS. Let me see—I think—

JOSEFA. (*Respectfully.*) Madame rang for her coffee at noon.

SEVIGNE. Is that correct?

MADAME BEAUREVERS. Yes, I think so.

(MADAME BEAUREVERS *turns to look at her, then back to Sevigne.* JOSEFA *instantly pantomimes furiously "driving," with steering wheel, horn-honking, etc.*)

SEVIGNE. At noon, Madame, Ostos had already left for Lyons.

(MORESTAN *stiffens,* JOSEFA *is tense with anticipation.*)

MADAME BEAUREVERS. I sent for Ostos *before* I rang for my coffee. I woke up at eleven and when I rang, it was the Cook who answered. I told her I wanted to see the chauffeur and *then* to send Josefa with my coffee. (*Turning to* JOSEFA.) I didn't ring that morning, did I, Josefa? It was the Cook who told you to take up my tray, wasn't it?

JOSEFA. (*Reluctantly.*) Yes, Madame.

(*She is let-down, as are they* ALL, *except for* MADAME BEAUREVERS, *who continues relentlessly.* JOSEFA *sits.*)

MADAME BEAUREVERS. You see, I am telling the truth. I took it for granted that my husband had taken the revolver from the car. He knew Ostos was maniacally jealous and even though he had planned to get him out of the way while he frolicked in the maid's room, I dare say it seemed wise not to leave a loaded gun where Ostos could get at it. That is certainly plausible, is it not?

SEVIGNE. (*Reluctantly.*) It would appear to be—

MADAME BEAUREVERS. Oh, I don't think he *meant* to kill Ostos, particularly since his date with Josefa was for eleven o'clock and he didn't believe that Ostos could conceivably get back until long after midnight. But— (*With a shrug.*) Ostos did manage to return soon after eleven, in time to find them together, and—you know what happened then.

SEVIGNE. Not an unlikely reconstruction, I must admit— (JOSEFA *is rocking with pain.*) How did you know your husband had arranged to meet Josefa at eleven o'clock that night, Madame?

MADAME BEAUREVERS. (*Uncertain.*) What do you mean?

SEVIGNE. I mean, how did you know that the rendezvous was to be at eleven o'clock that night?

MADAME BEAUREVERS. I didn't know. *You* told me. You asked me about a note he sent.

SEVIGNE. True, I did. But I said *ten o'clock*. (MADAME BEAUREVERS *is suddenly tense and alert.*) I mentioned the note twice, Madame, and each time—deliberately, I must admit—I said the date was for ten. But you knew the exact hour, didn't you, Madame?

MADAME BEAUREVERS. (*A touch of hoarseness now.*) It's not true. You said eleven. You must have said that.

SEVIGNE. (*Snapping it out.*) Morestan! Quickly—your notes!

MORESTAN. (*He flips back a few pages. Even he is animated. Reading.*) "On the day of the shooting, in the afternoon, your husband sent Josefa a note fixing a rendezous for ten o'clock that night. . . ." (*Looking up from his notes.*) And here again— (*Reading.*) "—if you had intercepted your husband's note and knew that he was to be in Josefa's room—at ten o'clock."

MADAME BEAUREVERS. (*Wildly.*) No! No!

SEVIGNE. (*Rises; attacking.*) Then how did you know the time that was in the note? Answer, Madame! It's crucial now because you are challenged by your own words—not mine or your husband's or any other witness's—your own. *How* did you know the time of the meeting? *How?*

MADAME BEAUREVERS. (*Weakly.*) I—I got the note— (SEVIGNE *nods, with no particular elation.*)

SEVIGNE. (*Matter of fact.*) And the rest of it?

MADAME BEAUREVERS. (*Weakly, but stubbornly.*) No! —no!—I deny it!

(SEVIGNE *sighs heavily. Waits a moment in which* MADAME BEAUREVERS *stares at him, then shifts her gaze uneasily. He goes to the door, opens it, beckons.*)

SEVIGNE. You, there—Guard!

(*As* MADAME BEAUREVERS *winces. The* GUARD *looms up behind him.*)

MADAME BEAUREVERS. (*Almost a whisper.*) You're arresting me?

SEVIGNE. (*At* C.) You should have time to think, Madame. (*Crosses to adjoining room, holds the door open.*) The affair can conceivably be regarded as a crime of passion, prompted by your husband's misconduct. Your lawyers will undoubtedly give you that advice.

MADAME BEAUREVERS. (*Hesitant.*) And you? (*Rises.*)

SEVIGNE. (*Wearily.*) I am not a judge, Madame, only a magistrate. (*Crosses* L. *to door.*)

(MADAME BEAUREVERS *rises finally, quite proud and erect. She goes to the open door and* SEVIGNE *gestures to the* GUARD *to follow.* MADAME BEAUREVERS *crosses* L.; GUARD *crosses* D. L. JOSEFA *rises.*)

SEVIGNE. Madame is not to be left alone.

MADAME BEAUREVERS. (*She pauses in the doorway to give him an appraising look. At* D. L.) Don't worry about my attempting suicide; I am not quite so obliging.

(*The* GUARD *follows her in, the door closes.*)

JOSEFA. (*At* L., *next to* L. *desk. Admiringly, genuinely.*) They've got class, eh? My God, if I had killed somebody I'd be trembling like a leaf. (*As an afterthought.*) Especially if I got caught. (SEVIGNE *has crossed* R. *and is slumped behind his desk, not with elation, just weariness.*) You were sensational! (*As* SEVIGNE *shrugs it off, she turns to* MORESTAN.) He was brilliant, wasn't he?

MORESTAN. Oh, yes—very.

SEVIGNE. (*He has written something on a pad, now tears it loose.*) Here, Morestan, get this counter-signed by the Chief Prosecutor.

MORESTAN. (*Crosses* C.; *bleakly.*) Right. (*Takes the paper, starts out.*)

SEVIGNE. (*To* JOSEFA.) That's an order for your release. When he brings it back, you're free.

JOSEFA. (*Calling after* MORESTAN.) Don't trip! (*Crosses Up. As the door closes; to* SEVIGNE, *in a curious tone.*) Free! (*Leans in despair.*)

SEVIGNE. Don't you like the idea?

JOSEFA. Oh, sure. That damn prison! (*Crosses* D. C.; *and then.*) I'll *really* be free. The man who loved me is dead; the man I loved— (*Bitterly.*) He thinks I'm some kind of marijuana bush. (*Wistfully.*) And if that's not free enough, I'm also out of a job! (*Sits* L. C.)

SEVIGNE. You'll get something else. (*At desk* R.)

JOSEFA. Oh, sure! With the reference I can expect from Madame—cashier in a bank! (*Gives* SEVIGNE *a sunny, reassuring smile.*) Don't worry—I've got plans.

SEVIGNE. Good.

JOSEFA. Strip-tease. (*Rises, crosses in* C. *Ignoring his pained look, she rattles on cheerfully.*) I heard about it in prison. Two of the girls in my cell told me. They said

I could make two hundred francs a night, anywhere in Montmartre. These two made even more than that—probably why they were in prison—but they told me where to go, who to ask for—everything. (SEVIGNE *crosses* D. R. JOSEFA *finally slowing down at* SEVIGNE'S *reaction. She follows.*) Oh?—don't you think it's a good idea?

SEVIGNE. It's not really for me to say—

JOSEFA. Oh, come on, you know more about me than anybody else except Miguel—and Monsieur Beaurevers and— (*Embarrassed.*) well, a few people. (*As* SEVIGNE *smiles.*) *Very* few.

SEVIGNE. I don't think you're like the girls you met in prison—

JOSEFA. (*Delighted.*) No? Truly?

SEVIGNE. Truly.

JOSEFA. After all you've heard about me—

SEVIGNE. After all I've heard.

JOSEFA. (*Marvelling.*) A man like you—I mean, you're practically a judge!

SEVIGNE. (*Wrily.*) Practically.

JOSEFA. (*Crosses* L. *a step.*) I don't know what to say. I'm bowled over. (*Warmly, eyes shining.*) Would you like it if—you know, you and I—well, you know— (*Impulsively.*) I mean, I like you, too. Otherwise, I wouldn't dream of it.

SEVIGNE. (*Startled.*) Josefa!

JOSEFA. I know that I would have been in the soup if not for you—and I *do* like you—and, well, you know so much about me already, so if you know a little more— (*She shrugs, smiles.*) So?

SEVIGNE. (*Crosses* L.; *gently.*) No. Thank you, Josefa, but no.

JOSEFA. You're sure? I mean, I know it's not a sensational offer, or anything, but I don't have much—

SEVIGNE. (*Earnestly.*) It is. Don't ever let anyone tell you it isn't. I'm touched and pleased that you should offer it— (*Smiling.*) But no, Josefa. (*Turns* R.)

JOSEFA. (*Follows.*) All right. But you've done so much— (*Suddenly, quite shyly.*) Would you like it if I *didn't* do the strip-tease?

SEVIGNE. Yes—very much.

JOSEFA. All right— (*Turns* C.; *cheerfully.*) In December—with those draughts—who needs it?

SEVIGNE. Get a good job, meet a nice fellow, settle down.

JOSEFA. A nice fellow! (*Doubtfully.*) You think I'm good luck? (*As he nods; doubtfully.*) I don't know. Nice fellows—you think they're all that easy to find? (*Crosses* L.; *her sunny smile flashes again.*) Now, *you're* nice. (*Appraisingly.*) In a way, you know, it's a pity—

SEVIGNE. Yes, it is. Luckily, I'm old enough to say: "Thank you, no"— (*With a smile.*) but I'm young enough to regret it. (*Crosses* L. *to her. Then, severely.*) And you—keep your mind on a job, a nice fellow. That's an order.

JOSEFA. Yes, sir.

(MORESTAN *enters, empty-handed, with a frustrated gesture. He looks as though he had been through a bad few minutes.*)

SEVIGNE. What is it? Where's the release order?

(MORESTAN *and* SEVIGNE *at* C.)

MORESTAN. On the Chief Prosecutor's desk.
SEVIGNE. Didn't he sign it?

(JOSEFA *is looking from one to the other as at a tennis match.*)

MORESTAN. Sign it? He wouldn't even *look* at it. (*He adds.*) I think he's willing to release *us*—but not *her*.

SEVIGNE. (*Grimly.*) I'll see about that. (*He exits quickly.*)

MORESTAN. (*Sitting* L. C.) Whew! (*Mops his fore-*

head.) Wait till he gets upstairs. The Chief's office is teeming with judges, deputies, ministers, high officials—all related to the Beaurevers.

JOSEFA. (*Crosses* C.) Will he— (*Pointing to the exit.*) Is he in trouble?

MORESTAN. Ha! (*Making it clear.*) H-A, with an exclamation mark.

JOSEFA. Because he got me out of trouble! (*Crosses* R.; *a wail.*) Oh, no!

MORESTAN. Don't worry. The Chief has these sullen periods but they never last more than a few years.

JOSEFA. What will they do to him?

MORESTAN. Oh, he'll live— (*With a shrug.*) Not as well, perhaps, as if he had followed orders—

JOSEFA. They won't make him a judge?

MORESTAN. A judge! Ha! H-A, with *two* exclamation marks.

JOSEFA. (*Wrathfully.*) It's my fault! Me and my stupid innocence! If I had any sense I'd be guilty and everyone would be better off!

(MORESTAN *sighs, as if this would be too good to be true.* JOSEFA *is slumped miserably in her chair. The* GUARD *comes to the door of the adjoining room.*)

GUARD. Monsieur—

(*The* GUARD *beckons to* MORESTAN, *who crosses to him. The* GUARD *whispers something,* MORESTAN *nods bleakly. The* GUARD *goes back in, the door closes.* MORESTAN *turns to his desk, takes pencils and notebook.*)

MORESTAN. Madame wishes to make a statement. When he gets back—if he gets back—tell him. (*He goes into the adjoining room.*)

(JOSEFA *fumbles in her purse for a cigarette, but before she can light it,* SEVIGNE *has entered.*)

SEVIGNE. (*Crosses in* C.) Where's Morestan?

JOSEFA. Inside—with Madame. She wanted to make a statement.

SEVIGNE. Yes, I thought she'd get around to that. (*Then he extends the document.*) Here is the order for your release—signed. (*He is surprised when* JOSEFA *retreats from him, her hands behind her back.*)

JOSEFA. No! No, I don't want it!

SEVIGNE. What's wrong with you? (*He tries to force the paper on her, she retreats.*)

JOSEFA. No! I refuse! (*She has backed as far as she can go.*) You're in trouble, because you got me out of trouble—

SEVIGNE. (*Sharply.*) That's none of your business!

JOSEFA. It is! Send her home! (*Pointing to the room.*) I'll confess. (*He stops, looking at her curiously.*) I don't mind—honest.

SEVIGNE. (*Curtly.*) I do.

JOSEFA. I was just putting on an act about the prison —it was fun, I *liked* it.

SEVIGNE. (*Crosses to her; softly, tenderly.*) You damn fool!

JOSEFA. (*Pleading.*) All her relatives—presidents and prime-ministers and deputies—why should you have all that lot on your hands? With me, even if they sent me to the guillotine, you wouldn't even get a complaint on a postcard.

SEVIGNE. Stop that! (*She just looks at him. He adds tenderly.*) Idiot!

JOSEFA. I know. I am. (*Then eagerly.*) I'll get into some trouble anyway—see if I don't. I'd much rather give you a nice confession. You'll get promoted—

SEVIGNE. Who's been telling you all this? Was it Morestan?

JOSEFA. No— (*Weakly.*) I guessed.

SEVIGNE. (*Crosses* L.) Now, listen: you owe me nothing. They gave me this shabby little room and a handful of puzzle pieces. And then the machinery worked—properly, for once—and it got put together. You just happened to be one of the pieces. (*With a smile.*) I'm glad of that.

JOSEFA. I'm glad you were running the machine. (*And then, almost a wail.*) But I want you to be a judge! (*Crosses* L. *to him.*)

SEVIGNE. I'll make it. Promise! (*He gives her the release order; she takes it reluctantly.*) I'll have someone see you out with that— (*Indicating the document. He goes to the entrance door, opens it, beckons.*) Guard!

JOSEFA. So—it's finished?

SEVIGNE. Finished.

JOSEFA. Oh, well— (*She looks him up and down in a lingering way.*)

SEVIGNE. (*Sternly.*) Josefa!

JOSEFA. Sorry— (*Apologetically.*) I wish I could give you *something*—a souvenir. (*She smiles delightedly, shaking loose the square of silk crumpled in her hand, and extending it to him shyly.*) Please. It's nothing, but it would be a keepsake. See—it's from the bullfights—the matador, and the bull, and everything. Miguel brought it to me last year from Bayonne. (*Urging it on him.*) Please.

SEVIGNE. All right. Thank you, Josefa. Thank you very much.

JOSEFA. (*Embarrassed.*) It's nothing.

(JOSEFA *and* SEVIGNE *shake hands; he turns to go into the adjoining room and* JOSEFA *starts for the door. She turns and finds him watching her. Holding up the handkerchief, he says:*)

SEVIGNE. Ole! Ole!

JOSEFA. Ole! Ole!

SEVIGNE. Remember, a good job, a nice fellow, you'll know how to make him happy.

JOSEFA. I hope I remember.

(*With one last look around while* SEVIGNE *watches*, JOSEFA *exits slowly.*)

CURTAIN

PROPERTIES
ACT ONE

Set Furniture:
1. Witness chair on Act I (onstage) marks
2. Bentwood chair (Up Left by Morestan's desk) on Act I (Upstage) marks
3. Caneback arm chair at far Up Left

On Sevigne's Desk (Stage Right) :
1. Fix File Folder
    a 4 written pages in 1st compartment
    b Photo of bullets in 2nd compartment
    c 1 written page in last compartment
2. 4 lawbooks on desk (3 open, 1 shut)
3. Eyeglasses on file folder
4. Pencils to the right of blotter
5. 4 Black notebooks at right of blotter
6. Ashtray, cigarette and matches in small file drawer
7. Place arrest order on blotter
8. Place telephone in position
9. Place pen and inkwell in position
10. Check desk drawer for handkerchief
11. Place single paper from wastebasket on floor

On Morestan's Desk (Stage Left)
1. Chalk
2. Black notebooks
3. Pencils

Offstage Prop Table (Up Center)
1. Notebook for Morestan

Check:
1. Calendar—Nov. 8
2. Pull out drawer next to calendar
3. Water pitcher and glasses (Pitcher and glass on Morestan's desk and glass on Sevigne's desk)

ACT TWO

Sevigne's Desk
1. Pile lawbooks on upstage end of desk
2. Put used handkerchief in drawer
3. Remove chalk and put it back on Morestan's desk

PROPERTIES

4. Replace Morestan's notebook on prop table
5. Put Release Order on blotter
6. Restore file folder and eyeglasses from Morestan's desk to Sevigne's desk
7. Place more paper from wastebasket on floor

Furniture
1. Move witness chair to Act II (offstage) marks
2. Move Bentwood chair (Up Left) to Act II (Downstage) marks

Check
1. Calendar—Nov. 10
2. Erasure of chalk drawing on floor

ACT THREE

Furniture
1. Witness chair on Act II marks
2. Bentwood chair (Up Left) to Act II marks
3. Caneback arm chair to Act III (Downstage) **marks**

HAND PROPS

Add:—For Act III only
  Transcript of Evidence (from the script)
    On Stage Left desk
  Release Order, On Stage Right Desk
  Sealed, Signed Documents, to be placed in the File of the Case, On Stage Right Desk
  Ashtray, On Desk Right Stage
  Pitcher of Water, Glass, On Desk Left Stage

Off Stage: Up Center

ACT I:
Cigarettes, Matches—Josefa
Compact, Lipstick—Antoinette
Handkerchief—Sevigne
Eyeglasses—Sevigne
Notebooks—Morestan

ACT II:
Newspaper clipping of a Photo—Josefa
Calendar change
Clean chalk off floor
Put papers on floor
Replace File, Eyeglasses on Sevigne's desk

ACT III:
Cigarettes, Matches—Sevigne
Release Order on Sevigne's desk